BIRD WATCHER'S
DIGEST

BUTTERFLIES

BACKYARD GUIDE

Identify • Watch • Attract • Nurture • Save

ERIN GETTLER

COOL
SPRINGS
PRESS
Home and Garden Experts™

MINNEAPOLIS, MINNESOTA

D0106887

Quarto is the authority on a wide range of topics.

Quarto educates, entertains and enriches the lives of our readers—enthusiasts and lovers of hands-on living.

www.quartoknows.com

© 2017 Quarto Publishing Group USA Inc.

First published in 2017 by Cool Springs Press, an imprint of Quarto Publishing Group USA Inc., 400 First Avenue North, Suite 400, Minneapolis, MN 55401 USA. Telephone: (612) 344-8100 Fax: (612) 344-8692

quartoknows.com

Visit our blogs at quartoknows.com

Cool Springs Press titles are also available at discounts in bulk quantity for industrial or sales-promotional use. For details contact the Special Sales Manager at Quarto Publishing Group USA Inc., 400 First Avenue North, Suite 400, Minneapolis, MN 55401 USA.

10 9 8 7 6 5 4 3 2 1

ISBN: 978-1-59186-675-6

Library of Congress Cataloging-in-Publication Data

Names: Gettler, Erin, 1982- , author.
Title: Bird watcher's digest butterflies backyard guide : identify, watch, attract, nurture, save / Erin Gettler.
Other titles: Butterflies backyard guide | Bird watcher's digest.
Description: Minneapolis, MN : Cool Springs Press, 2017. | Includes index.
Identifiers: LCCN 2016030319 | ISBN 9781591866756 (sc)
Subjects: LCSH: Butterflies--North America--Identification. | Butterfly watching--North America.
Classification: LCC QL548 .G48 2017 | DDC 595.78/9097--dc23
LC record available at https://lccn.loc.gov/2016030319

Acquiring Editor: Jordan Wiklund
Project Manager: Alyssa Bluhm
Art Director: Brad Springer
Layout: Danielle Smith-Boldt

Printed in China

MIX

Paper from responsible sources

FSC® C016973

www.fsc.org

DEDICATION & ACKNOWLEDGMENTS

DEDICATION
For Joe, of course.

ACKNOWLEDGMENTS
I am full of gratitude to everyone whose words, hands, and heart touched this book along its path from pixels to pages.

First, thanks go to Bill Thompson III and *Bird Watcher's Digest* for inviting me to play in the sandbox of this book series. I'll always be grateful for the opportunity to roll around in words and butterflies for a whole year, and to have a book to show for it in the end.

Naturalists learn from those who have walked the trails before them, and I'd be nowhere without the knowledge of writers and naturalists who first sparked my curiosity through the pages of their own books and guides. I'm indebted to their curiosity and generosity, and I hope this book is a worthy addition to their significant contributions.

For encouragement and advice, I couldn't have asked for a better cheering section. Julie, Ernie, Tim, and Seabrooke, your thoughts and experience have been invaluable in building this book. Special thanks to my favorite Internet friends, the Nosy Bs, who let me tap their enthusiasm and love whenever I was running dry. Between Illinois and New York, I have the best families a writer could ask for. I can't wait to put this book in your hands (signed, of course) and answer all your butterfly questions! My parents get all the credit for my writing habit, which started with the gift of a blank composition book and the invitation to fill it up with my own stories when I was seven. Thank you, from my heart.

Finally, I owe a shelfful of trophies to my husband, Joe, for helping me over the course of this past wild year: Best Partner, Best Editor, Best Encourager, Most Patient Spouse, Best Brainstormer, Best Ice-Cream-and-Tea Getter, Best at Suggesting Takeout When We'd Both Run out of Time, Best at Convincing Me I Could Really Do This. There's no way this book would be here without his support.

CONTENTS

Foreword

In this age of complete immersion in technology, it's nice to be reminded that the natural world is full of living, moving, three-dimensional wonders and splendors for us, if we only take the time to look. The first time I met author Erin Gettler, she was stooping low in a grassy field along the Maine coast, taking a photograph of a butterfly. We were there as part of a weeklong nature camp—she as a participant and I as an instructor—but by the end of that week, she'd easily taught me more about butterflies than I'd taught her about birds. She is the ideal author and guide to take us on a journey of discovery among the butterflies— nature's silent, flying jewels.

Erin's own inspiration for a lifelong love of nature came while gardening with her mother in their small-town backyard in northern Illinois. Growing some garden plants from seed, Erin would, as she says, "go out twenty-five times a day to see if they'd sprouted yet." While checking on the garden's progress, she "noticed some bugs and other stuff" and went to her collection of nature books to help put names on the creatures and plants she was seeing. Soon, birds, butterflies, and botany were her passion.

Butterflies are not only habitat specialists; many of them rely on a single plant species for their reproduction. These host plants are critical to maintaining healthy butterfly populations, and we humans can play a helpful role in preserving natural diversity of both plants and pollinators by using native plants in our yards and gardens.

Through the pages of this book, Erin Gettler joins a long line of naturalist authors hoping to inspire readers—especially young readers—to think about the important connection between healthy habitats and a healthy planet. And along the way, we can gaze in wonder at the butterflies and other wildlife drawn to our gardens through our thoughtful stewardship.

—Bill Thompson, III
Publisher, *Bird Watcher's Digest*

INTRODUCTION

Children instinctively understand the fascination of butterflies: the big, flashy wings; the squishy, wiggly caterpillars; the alchemy of metamorphosis that transforms those tiny eating machines into graceful, flower-sipping adults. Some of us never grow out of our fascination with butterflies, thanks to unexpected, unforgettable encounters in our adulthood. Butterflies bring some of the brightest bits of the natural world right into our own backyards. A quick tour of North America's seven hundred–plus species of butterflies reveals immense diversity, from fingernail-sized scraps of blues to subtly beautiful brown satyrs to hand-width, yellow-and-black striped swallowtails, many of which are common enough to be found in parks and neighborhoods across the continent. If you've ever spotted a butterfly and wondered what it's called and how you can see more like it, this is the book for you.

A painted lady butterfly.

WHY WATCH BUTTERFLIES?

After plants, there's hardly a more accessible entry into learning about the natural world than butterflies. They're found in nearly every habitat, they're pretty, many species are easy to approach, and they have a fascinating and easy-to-observe life cycle. A child can quickly learn the names of the few dozen common species that live in his or her neighborhood.

Butterflies open up a whole world of questions and offer a lifelong return of answers.

Even beyond satisfying those sparks of curiosity, there's a great deal of value in simply paying attention to the natural world around us. Butterflies are much heartier than we give them credit for, and yet many species face the threat of extinction because the habitats they evolved to thrive in are disappearing. Getting to know butterflies, and sharing their incredible lives with family and friends, helps secure their place in our hearts, and in the planet's future.

WHAT IS BUTTERFLY WATCHING?

The question of "what is butterfly watching?" is not as silly as it looks at first glance. Much like bird watching, the study of butterflies was originally a matter of capturing, preserving, and collecting butterfly specimens to study up close and at leisure. Wild-flying butterflies can be difficult to observe with the naked eye: they move quickly, evade perceived predators, and dive out of sight when they feel threatened. That's why butterfly aficionados of the past carried large nets and equipment for quickly killing and preserving their captured specimens. The butterflies were carefully prepared and pinned with their wings spread open to reveal their colors and patterns for future study. These insect collections provided valuable information about butterfly identification, variation among each species, habitat, and range that inform our understanding of butterflies today. Now, we have more options to enjoy living butterflies in our gardens and in their own natural habitats, thanks in part to innovations that made the related hobby of bird watching accessible to everyone.

Birding transformed when binoculars became powerful and lightweight enough to replace the need to use guns to bring birds close enough to study. Modern field guides completed the renaissance. In 1934, ornithologist Roger Tory Peterson published a book that systematically showed how to tell one bird from another based on *field marks*—characteristic markings of each species—of the living bird from a distance. Butterflies didn't get the same treatment until quite recently, when close-focusing binoculars became available and allowed naturalists to view and magnify butterflies from as close as 6 feet. From this range, an observer can appreciate miniscule patterns and colors, as well as enjoy watching the butterfly engage in natural behaviors. And extending the concept of field marks to butterfly identification has made it easier to recognize butterflies and skippers in natural postures, where wings are held closed or collapsed, instead of spread flat. Butterfly gardening and butterfly field guides, based on the observations of past natural historians, bring butterflies even closer to us, expanding their fascination beyond the range of dedicated butterfly scholars and into the reach of anyone whose heart leaps after a pair of bright, fluttering wings.

Butterfly watching is as simple as watching butterflies do what butterflies do. This guide will help you hang names on many of the butterflies you encounter in your garden or local park. Don't be in the least bit surprised, however, when knowing a butterfly's name catalyzes your curiosity. Soon you'll want to know even more.

GETTING STARTED

The first step in butterfly watching is knowing how and where to find butterflies. Nothing will whet your appetite for watching butterflies better than finding some in the first place! Gardens with plenty of blooming flowers are your best bet for immediate butterfly gratification, especially in June and July. Your own yard or a friend's may be a good place to start if it's full of flowering plants, but if not, try the nearest public garden or arboretum. Otherwise, look for open, natural fields in parks or preserves throughout the summer when the plants are at peak bloom. High-quality habitats such as these support many butterfly species at the same time, offering good opportunities to see different kinds of butterflies in one place.

Sunny dirt roads often boast a buffet of blooming wildflowers, making them excellent places to seek butterflies.

Butterflies are easy to spot in gardens and on concentrated clusters of flowers, but in other situations it may take some practice to tune your "butterfly eyes," especially for the tiniest butterflies. Practice sweeping your gaze around and over the vegetation as you walk down a path, paying careful attention to small movements. Eventually you'll train your eyes to quickly recognize the flight speed and patterns of butterflies, and even to tell the difference from other large flying insects such as dragonflies and bees that often share habitat with butterflies. Once your eyes land on a butterfly, follow it quietly from a short distance until it lands to feed or bask. Approach perched butterflies slowly, and try not to cast a shadow. Movement and sudden shade send butterflies into flight faster than you can blink.

Flipping through guides like this one will help you figure out what to look for when you do spot a butterfly. You'll grow familiar with the different groups of butterflies, from blues to sulphurs to commas to skippers, and that will help you narrow down what sort of butterfly you're looking at. Teach yourself how to recognize ten butterflies from your area. This will help you place any unfamiliar butterfly into the proper group (sulphur, copper, fritillary, for example), and also give you a whole suite of criteria to compare the new butterfly to: Is it smaller than a monarch? Does it have tails like a swallowtail? Does it have a pattern similar to an American lady? The first ten butterflies you learn will put you on the right path to learning the next ten, and the next ten after that.

EQUIPMENT

The most important equipment for the butterfly watcher is your own power of observation, but some things can make it easier to appreciate the nuances of

butterfly markings. One of the most helpful aids is a pair of close-focusing binoculars. Look for a pair of binoculars that focuses within at least 8 feet. Many of the best options will focus within 6 feet. Binoculars are described using a two-number formula, such as 7 × 25. The first number is the lenses' magnification power (7 × 25 binoculars

A pair of close-focusing binoculars is one of the best tools for butterfly watching.

magnify the image seven times). The second number is the diameter in millimeters of the objective (large) lens. For butterfly watching, a lower magnification power, such as 7 or 8, is preferable, and a larger objective measurement, such as 36 or 42, will let in more light and provide you with more visual clues about the butterflies you spot.

A magnifying glass or folding hand lens is also useful, especially when looking at

Hold hand lenses close to your subject and move your eyes to the lens for the best magnification.

caterpillars and eggs. These typically magnify your subject anywhere from three to twenty times. Managing the right distance between your eyes, the lens, and the subject takes a little practice. Hold the lens as close to your eye as possible. Then move your subject closer until it comes into focus—or move yourself closer to the object in question! If you can get close enough, hand lenses can also be useful for looking at adult butterflies. You can use binoculars as magnifiers in a pinch by turning them around and looking through the larger objective lens at your subject.

Many naturalists use notebooks to draw pictures, describe findings, and record details such as the plants they see butterflies and caterpillars feeding on. Notes are also useful if you're not sure what you're looking at. Write down everything you observe about an unknown butterfly or caterpillar in the moment. A lot of important details tend to leak out of memory on the way to a computer or your field guides! Some people also keep lists of the butterflies they see, organized by year or lifetime.

A digital camera is another very helpful recording tool. Cameras with zoom lenses let you freeze distant butterflies before they fly away, hopefully revealing the colors and patterns you'll need to identify your subject. I've also used my smartphone camera to secure important identification shots. Without a zoom lens, you'll need to practice stealthily creeping up on butterflies to get close enough for good pictures, but several species are very patient about having their pictures taken.

A large butterfly cage with mesh walls provides air circulation for butterflies and caterpillars.

Butterfly beauty shots can be a pleasant by-product of documentary photography, or they can be the main goal for artistic photographers.

If you wish to raise caterpillars to adulthood, you will need a cage of some kind. Large, pop-up mesh cages with zippers provide plenty of room for newly emerged adults to stretch their wings, and the finely woven fabric prevents small caterpillars from escaping while allowing air to circulate freely. Large aquarium tanks will also work well, but be sure the cover allows plenty of air circulation. Avoid keeping caterpillars in jars—even if you punch holes in the lid. Jars aren't large enough for newly emerged adult butterflies to stretch their wings without damage, and caterpillars can slice themselves up on the sharp edges of the holes.

BUILD YOUR KNOWLEDGE

Over time and with practice, your knowledge of butterfly species and behaviors will expand significantly. The trick is to keep looking. This guide will help you become familiar with many common species that live in your area, but it only covers 55 North American species out of approximately 725 total species. Once you've mastered these, you may want more information from guides that include more species. The options for advanced butterfly guides increase all the time. Borrow some from your local library to figure out which one works best for you, and then purchase one you like to dog-ear and mark up—or look for apps for your smartphone.

Hands-on (and eyes-on) experience is the best teacher, though. Visiting the same habitat frequently throughout the butterfly season will help you get a feel for how butterfly populations wax and wane throughout the year. One's personal, often-visited location is called a *patch* among naturalists, and the practice of visiting and carefully observing your patch over time is one of the most useful disciplines for learning about your local wildlife. You may also want to expand your searches in habitats off the beaten track, where you may find an even greater variety of butterflies in your area.

You may also want to delve deeper into butterfly life cycles by finding and rearing caterpillars. You can learn a great deal from each individual caterpillar, including its food preferences, habits, and growing periods. Even though the caterpillar does most of the work, releasing healthy adult butterflies is quite an accomplishment.

Many local natural history organizations—including museums, chapters of the Audubon Society or Sierra Club, and nature preservation societies—host field trips and informational talks led by naturalists and other experts. Take advantage of their expertise and soak up as much knowledge as you can. If your local organization doesn't yet offer butterfly walks, request that they be added to the program, and be sure to participate, and bring friends! You'll learn how to see and understand butterflies in ways you never have before.

TEN TIPS FOR GETTING STARTED

1. Binoculars will help you enjoy butterflies that are too skittish to approach closely. Practice following moving butterflies with your bare eyes, and then lifting the binoculars to your eyes when the butterfly perches.

2. Learn the butterfly groups before focusing on the individual species. This way, you won't get hung up if you don't know the species right away. Instead, if you can tell it's a sulphur, you can check that section in the guide later to compare the different species.

3. When you find a new butterfly, observe the big features first before moving on to the fine details. Take note of the butterfly's size, shape, and primary colors. Then look for field marks such as tails, eyespots, scattered markings, bars, etc. With time, you'll be able to recognize familiar species in an instant without referring to a checklist of field marks.

4.   Butterflies are most active in the afternoon. They soak up sunlight to conserve energy in the morning and take wing in the heat of the day.

5.   Early season butterflies such as mourning cloaks, commas, and spring azures bask in patches of sunshine on cool spring days.

6.   Check mud patches, stream edges, puddles, and animal dung for puddling butterflies. These are often the best spots to see dozens or more butterflies at a time.

7.   Tune in to small movements in your peripheral vision to spot butterflies before they disappear. Butterflies move fast, and sometimes you only get a glimpse as they fly away!

8.   If you find a popular nectar plant or puddling spot, stick around for a while. You'll see many different butterflies and skippers come and go, and probably recognize quite a few of them.

9.   Male butterflies on patrol tend to concentrate along trails and streams. Keep your eyes peeled for individuals "pacing" up and down the path.

10.   Start small when adding butterfly-friendly landscaping to your yard and add new beds and plants over time. Group nectar sources and host plants in large clusters. Butterflies see masses of plants and color better than individual plants.

HOW TO USE THIS BOOK

This guide includes profiles of 55 common butterfly species in North America. Some butterflies are common across the continent, but most have more limited ranges. Butterflies included here have large ranges that span over two or more regions. You'll note that there are fewer western-specific species than eastern or continental species. This is because the mountain-and-basin geology of the Rocky Mountains splits up the ranges of a huge variety of western butterflies, so more species are in the west, but fewer are common over large areas.

The featured species are arranged by taxonomic families, so butterflies that are related appear in the same section. This will help you compare different-but-similar butterflies to better learn how to tell them apart.

Each species profile includes one large photograph of the butterfly and one inset photograph of either the caterpillar or an additional identification picture showing alternate wing patterns. The written descriptions include answers to butterfly lovers' questions, including:

- **How do I identify them?** A description of the size, shape, patterns, and distinguishing features of the butterfly and its caterpillar, as well as how to differentiate it from similar butterflies.

- **Where do I find them?** The butterfly's range and habitat preferences.

- **What can I do to attract them?** Information on caterpillar host plants, adult food preferences, and tips on landscaping that appeals to the adult butterfly.

- **Life cycle,** which describes the time of year when the butterfly is active, how many generations it produces, how it spends the winter, and other interesting facts about the butterfly's life.

The **AT A GLANCE** chart gives a quick look at the butterfly's habitats and flight season, as well as other attributes that will help you find and recognize it.

AT A GLANCE	
HABITAT:	Open areas; woods and forest edges
PREDOMINANT COLORS:	Black, blue, orange
SEASON MOST OFTEN SEEN:	Spring through summer
MIGRATORY:	No

You can read this book cover to cover, flip through the profiles, or search out specific butterflies. The more time you spend with the butterflies, on the page and outdoors, the faster you'll learn them. Let's get started!

Creating Habitat

ATTRACTING BUTTERFLIES TO YOUR BACKYARD

It doesn't take much to get the attention of passing butterflies—one nectar-filled plant in a pot can sometimes do the trick. Butterflies need a little more from a habitat than flowers, though, and with natural spaces declining all over, they could use more habitat . . . period. Creating a butterfly haven isn't complicated, and the results, both winged and rooted, are beautiful. And by making your yard butterfly friendly, you'll help keep butterflies flying for good. In this chapter, let's talk about the butterfly life cycle and what butterflies need from their habitat from caterpillar through adulthood. You'll learn how to design your space to appeal to a wide variety of butterflies, from flowers to shelter to food sources for caterpillars, so you can watch the next generation of butterflies take flight right before your eyes.

NURTURE: LIFE CYCLE AND BEHAVIORS

A blooming garden will encourage adult butterflies to fuel up as they pass through, but if you want to see the full suite of fascinating butterfly behaviors and encourage them to stick around, you'll want to appeal to butterflies in all phases of life. Understanding the butterfly life cycle is key to designing a backyard habitat that will invite a wide variety of butterflies and encourage them to stay, court, mate, and lay eggs, which is where the whole butterfly story begins.

EGG

You see a butterfly hovering around a leaf, perching momentarily, and then flitting away to examine the next plant. This is most likely a female butterfly depositing an egg, and if you watch closely enough, you may catch the act itself. Each species has its own egg-laying regimen: some species lay only a single egg at a time; others deposit a cluster. The location of the egg is often species-specific too: the female may glue the egg to the top or underside of a leaf or on a stem, or deposit an egg in leaf litter near the host plant, but not on it. Caterpillars of many butterfly species can only feed on specific plant species, so female butterflies of these species range far and wide to find the correct, healthy host plants for their precious eggs.

Butterfly eggs are works of art: tiny crystalline sculptures that invite close examination with a magnifying glass if you find them (check spots where those fluttering females land!). The eggshell is also typically the caterpillar's first meal after hatching, which usually occurs within a few days of being laid. Eating the eggshell hides the first evidence of a caterpillar's existence from predators such as birds and other insects.

Butterfly eggs.

A monarch caterpillar.

CATERPILLAR

Caterpillars hatch from tiny capsules, so it's no surprise they start out almost invisibly small and well camouflaged. As they grow, they shed their tight skins and emerge larger, often with different colors and patterns. Each of these molt phases is called an *instar*, and caterpillars usually grow through four to five instars before they pupate to complete their metamorphosis.

A caterpillar's primary job is to eat, and they deploy impressive defensive strategies to deter predators so they can focus on the next bite. Sharp-eyed songbirds, in particular, depend on butterfly and moth caterpillars to feed their chicks, so caterpillars have evolved a broad arsenal of weapons and camouflage. Some build nests out of silk threads, similar to spider silk, or wrap leaves around themselves to hide. Some manufacture toxins from the food they eat so that they taste bitter or upset predators' stomachs—these species' bright orange, black, or yellow patterns warn that they are bad to eat. Others sport spiky armor or irritating bristles. And some caterpillars are deceptively colored with patterns disguising them as mottled leaves or twigs, or even threatening snakes.

🦋 BUTTERFLIES 101

How can you find caterpillars if they're so good at hiding? Look for their poop! Caterpillars process a lot of food through their digestive systems, and they don't move very far. Their blackish, gritty feces, called *frass*, sometimes collects in leaves and on the ground below them. If you find the ground below a tree covered in frass, look up, but keep your mouth closed. You may have found a tree full of caterpillars!

PUPA

After a caterpillar completes the last instar, it transitions into the pupal phase during which the caterpillar metamorphoses into the adult butterfly inside a protective shell called a chrysalis. Each butterfly species has strategies to hide or disguise itself during this immobile phase, when it's even more vulnerable to being eaten than before. The pupa may hang head-down, or lean away from a twig or stem with a band of silk wrapped around its middle like a belt holding the chrysalis upright. Some make a cocoon of silk inside a leaf or fastened to a tree, and others simply drop down into leaf litter or dig under the dirt to complete their transformation undisturbed.

Inside the chrysalis, the future-butterfly's genes are busy coordinating a massive reorganization of all the biological material that *was* a caterpillar, using the fuel stored from its days as an

A monarch chrysalis.

eating machine. Metamorphosis transforms the caterpillar's organs, muscles, and systems to suit the requirements of adulthood as a flying reproductive creature— an adult butterfly. The pupa phase can span a few weeks to months for a species that overwinters in its chrysalis.

ADULT

When metamorphosis is complete, the chrysalis contains a fully developed adult butterfly. The last step is the most dramatic: the chrysalis splits open, and a bedraggled creature with a swollen body and crumpled wings emerges. It hardly looks like a butterfly, but it will rather quickly. The wings start soft so they don't tear as the butterfly crawls out of the chrysalis, and once the new butterfly is free,

An adult monarch butterfly.

the engorged abdomen starts pumping its extra fluid into the wings to spread them out in their final form. The wings' internal framework stiffens within minutes, and the butterfly's exoskeleton hardens. The butterfly may rest a while after this exhausting event, slowly pumping its new wings for the first time in its life, but soon enough it will launch from its perch to complete its final mission: finding mates and reproducing.

Butterfly species emerge as adults at specific times in the year, and they're active for a few weeks before they die. These brief active cycles are called *flight periods*, and some species may have more than one flight period annually, with a new generation of adults for each one. The species profiles in the pages to come include information about each butterfly's flight period and whether they produce multiple generations each year.

Butterflies, like this eastern comma, bask in the sun to warm themselves and conserve energy.

BEHAVIORS

Throughout their lives, butterflies engage in behaviors to help them survive and successfully find mates. Some behaviors are so characteristic of certain butterfly species that they can be used to find and recognize them. But just as importantly, familiarity with butterfly behavioral needs can guide the choices you make in creating your backyard butterfly habitat.

The second priority of a caterpillar, after eating, is not getting eaten. In addition to armor, camouflage, and disguises, some caterpillars use threatening or startling displays to convince predators to leave them alone. Caterpillars from the swallowtail family have a bright orange, forked appendage, called an *osmeterium*—usually tucked away behind their heads—that quickly unfurls when the caterpillar is threatened. This organ emits a nasty odor, and, combined with the eyespots that some swallowtail caterpillars wear, may startle birds into thinking that they've accidentally approached a snake instead of a meal. Some caterpillars release obnoxious odors or fluids when disturbed. Other caterpillars writhe furiously when picked up or touched, and a few are even capable of making high-pitched squeals by forcing air through their respiratory tubes.

A lot of adult butterfly behaviors are likely familiar to you, though you may not have thought about their significance before. Basking—when a butterfly perches in the sunshine—is a strategy to conserve energy, and it comes in two flavors: open-winged and closed-winged. Butterflies typically have a species-specific preference between the two options. Maintain sunny spaces in your yard, with bushes and low plants to perch on, to encourage butterflies to bask where you can see them.

If you've ever noticed a butterfly rush out to chase and batter everything with wings, you've witnessed a male butterfly defending his territory. Male butterflies have some of the most obvious behaviors, and that's intentional. They want females to find them. Some patrol a territorial patch or a path in the woods, or they may perch on a high point from which they can fly out and chase away intruders. Not all males have territories. Another male behavior is called *hilltopping*: the butterfly finds a high, clear spot, often a bare hilltop, and flies around it hoping for a female to spot him as she passes by. A puddle or mud patch may attract dozens and sometimes hundreds of male butterflies who feed on the minerals and salts in the damp soil, a behavior creatively named *puddling*.

Clouded sulphurs sip minerals from the soil of a gravel road, engaging in a behavior called puddling.

BUTTERFLIES 101

One of my favorite things to do is to slowly approach a perching butterfly, extend a finger, and see if I can coax the tiny winged creature to climb aboard. Some butterflies will land on people to sip their sweat. You can also pour water on the bare ground and wait quietly for butterflies to stop by to sip the damp nutrients out of the soil, or try saturating a small piece of paper towel with your saliva and leave it on a leaf for the same effect.

You can easily create habitat conditions that encourage males to take up residence and set up territories, especially since they're mostly looking for the same thing that female butterflies are looking for: excellent food sources for their caterpillars. Read on to learn how to choose the best plants to grow for caterpillars and how to feed adult butterflies too.

After spending weeks feeding on garden carrots, a black swallowtail caterpillar prepares to pupate, hanging by a silk thread.

ATTRACT: FOOD

Butterfly food does more than simply provide energy. A caterpillar's diet may also provide toxins or bitter-tasting compounds that it can use as defense against predators, as well as the stored fuel that will power the caterpillar's metamorphosis as it transforms into an adult butterfly. Additionally, the proteins a caterpillar eats will continue to support the adult butterfly throughout the rest of its life.

BUTTERFLIES 101

A handful of caterpillars around the world trade vegetarianism for a carnivore's lifestyle as entomological wolves in sheep's clothing. They use camouflage to sneak into colonies of aphids or ant larvae and prey on them undetected. Our sole carnivorous caterpillar in North America is the harvester (see page 68).

As adults, butterflies need food that provides energy and minerals. Most of us are familiar with butterflies that feed on flower nectar, but some groups of butterflies, such as tortoiseshells and commas, eat tree sap, fermented fruit, and animal dung.

Butterfly species use diet strategies somewhere on a spectrum from generalist (not picky, able to feed on many kinds of food) to specialist (strictly able to feed on only one or two kinds of food). Specialist strategies are used more by caterpillars, some of which can only feed on one specific host plant or plant family. Monarchs are a famous example of a species with a specialized caterpillar diet: monarch caterpillars only eat plants in the milkweed family, from which they gain bitter-tasting toxins that deter predators. Caterpillars closer to the generalist side of the spectrum may be able to feed on leaves from trees and plants belonging to several different families. Most of our adult butterflies do not have very strict dietary requirements beyond diet type (sap versus nectar), although some prefer certain sources or plant species over others. Adult butterfly nectar preferences and host plants for their caterpillars are included in the species profiles.

Many woodland butterflies—such as the ladies, tortoiseshells, and satyrs—feed on sap, fermented fruit, and animal dung, instead of flower nectar. In forests, there are fewer blooming flowers after the first flush of spring, so these butterflies specialize in alternative food sources. A sunny yard full of blooming flowers won't appeal to most woodland butterflies. However, you can attract some of the more widely ranging species by setting out plates of soft, juicy fruit in your yard, or hanging fruit in the cages used to provide suet for birds. Oranges and bananas work well, but you can experiment to see what attracts butterflies in your area. Spring and early summer are the most likely seasons for these butterflies to be wandering through your yard.

One important consideration when choosing plants for your yard is caterpillars' dependence on native plant species. Insects and plants have been engaged in chemical warfare for millennia, with plants producing toxins meant to repel herbivores and insects evolving ways to overcome those toxins over and over again. Plant and insect species with long histories—those that evolved in the same location—exist in a tenuous balance, each able to succeed despite the toll of the other's defense or offense. On the other hand, many popular landscaping plants are bug-resistant imports from other continents. We've historically chosen these plants to decorate our yards in part because our native insects have not evolved to overcome their defenses. Imported landscaping plants don't get chewed nearly as badly as native plants. Unfortunately, this means residential areas are deserts as far as native pollinators are concerned, and as new developments eat up more natural space, fewer and fewer wild spaces and native host plants remain.

Caring about butterflies, and all the insect species we depend on to keep ecosystems in balance, means that we need to make a mental shift in how we think about our yards. If we see our properties as space we share with insects—if we reconceive human space as habitat for wildlife too—we can work to increase natural areas that will support butterflies and other important pollinators. Using some native plants in place of imported exotic species goes a long way toward increasing available habitat, instead of using it up.

NURTURE: SHELTER AND OVERWINTERING

Residents in the southern United States and Mexico have the pleasure of butterflies year-round, but those of us further north can't help but notice their sudden absence when the temperatures drop. Even in the summer, it's clear that butterflies are creatures of warmth and sunlight: in the middle of August, they're most active during hot, still afternoons.

We know that many butterfly species migrate much like birds, spending their winters in warmer areas where the physical demands for survival are not so intense and spreading north in the spring and summer when they can easily meet their climate and nutritional needs. But like many other creatures, some butterfly species have evolved strategies to help survive winter without having to relocate. These species spend winter in a suspended metabolic state called *diapause*, similar to hibernation in mammals, in which to save energy they do not eat, move, or develop. Diapause can occur at any life stage, and each overwintering species passes the season in a specific stage—as caterpillars, pupae, or butterflies. There are advantages to emerging from diapause in each phase. Eggs and caterpillars wake in the spring to new, tender growth that is easy to eat and convert into

Look carefully at the undersides of host-plant leaves, like this stand of ready-to-bloom common milkweed, for eggs and young caterpillars.

rapid growth. Pupae and adults who emerge in the spring can take advantage of abundant nectar from blooming plants or flowing sap, and adults can time their egg laying for the hatching caterpillars' emergence to coincide with early spring and summer plant growth.

You can make your yard a year-round butterfly paradise with landscaping and maintenance choices that provide butterflies shelter at all life stages. Caterpillars, eggs, and pupae typically overwinter in leaves or at the bases of their host plants, tucked into the shelter of the past year's growth. Leaving plants and dead leaves intact ensures that any eggs, caterpillars, and pupae buried inside will survive the winter snug under a leafy blanket. It also means you're not raking away and composting next year's butterflies!

Some adult butterflies also overwinter in leaf litter, but many species creep into crevices in tree trunks, fallen logs, or into cracks in the earth. Some of these butterflies, such as the mourning cloak and the comma, are well camouflaged to blend in with tree bark and leaf litter. For adult overwintering butterflies, availability of these kinds of sheltered spots is the most important thing.

ATTRACT: CREATING HABITAT

As we've seen, butterflies need more than just food. Habitat is the full scope of the environment that butterflies require for shelter, food for caterpillars and adults, and reproducing future generations. While some people convert their entire yards to gardens and shelters to support butterflies, you can start with small changes that immediately improve your yard's habitat potential and increase the number of butterfly visitors you'll see.

Before talking about plants, though, there are important things to think about with regard to your tolerance for a bit of rambunctious, natural mess in your yard. If you add native plants with the intention of feeding butterflies, some of the plants will likely end up looking a little raggedy as insect larvae of all kinds chow down. This is a good thing! It means your habitat upgrades are successful as far as your guests are concerned. You'll also want to consider foregoing fall cleanup, at least in some areas of your yard, to provide insulation and shelter for overwintering butterflies.

Nearly every landscaping strategy can be customized to increase your property's appeal to butterflies. Even formal gardens can host butterflies and their caterpillars as long as they include host plants that appeal to species that occur in your region,

A swallowtail butterfly stops to feed on joe-pye weed.

but they may be a little less pristine thanks to their dual purpose use. Many butterflies aren't picky about their surroundings at all. I once hosted a family of six black swallowtail caterpillars in a single potted parsley on my apartment stoop, right next to a blacktop parking lot. The caterpillars nibbled the parsley down to stubs, but the plant bounced back and the caterpillars moved on to pupate after they finished.

The spectrum of yard habitats for butterflies includes everything from potted nectar sources and formal landscaping with native plants to dedicated butterfly gardens and all the way to wild prairie yards. You should consider how natural your area is to start with (if you live in a wooded neighborhood, for example, you can use techniques to improve your yard's appeal as a forest habitat). Also consider your proximity to other natural habitats such as marshes, meadows, old fields and the like, and your own landscaping preferences.

Many native plants do very well in cultivation and as elements of formal gardens. It only takes a little extra thought to replace an invasive burning bush with an equally stunning native blueberry, which is a shrub that does very well in hedges, borders, and foundation plantings, and offers loads of fall color.

The most important factor when landscaping for butterflies is to plan to have something blooming spring, summer, and fall. Spring-flying butterflies will avoid your yard if it has nothing to offer them, and likewise for late-summer and fall flyers. The chart on the next page offers a list of native plant species sorted by region, growth habit, and blooming season that will help you choose the right plant for your area. If you can, plant groups of the same species, or cluster plants together that share the same blooming period. Concentrating food sources like this makes it easier for butterflies to find them without expending too much energy.

Each of the following butterfly profiles includes information on the species' caterpillar host plants, if known. You can plant known caterpillar hosts if you wish to attract certain butterfly species, or you can plant a variety of host plants and see what happens. Try to plant several specimens of each host plant if possible. I once found three nice, fat monarch caterpillars on a single common milkweed plant I'd tucked into my community garden bed. The caterpillars ate every leaf on that milkweed plant without satisfying their ravenous appetites, and I had to relocate them after they'd devoured the ill-advised host plant selection. If you plant it, they will come, sometimes in droves!

BUTTERFLIES 101

Avoid pesticides altogether if you are trying to encourage butterflies to use your yard. Butterflies are not immune to the effects of insecticides and will die or fail to reproduce if they encounter pesticides intended for other species.

NATIVE NECTAR PLANTS FOR BUTTERFLIES

FLOWERS			
Common Name	**Scientific Name**	**Blooming Season**	**Region**
Columbine	*Aquilegia* spp.	Spring	All
Marsh marigold	*Caltha palustris*	Spring	All
Birdfoot, blue, sagebrush, little white & other violets	*Viola* spp.	Spring–Summer	All
Bee balms and bergamot	*Monarda* spp.	Summer	All
Blazing stars	*Liatris* spp.	Summer	All
Common yarrow	*Achillea millefolium*	Summer	All
Hoary vervain, blue vervain and other verbenas	*Verbena stricta, V. hastata, V.* spp.	Summer	All
Milkweeds	*Asclepias* spp.	Summer	All
Pearly everlasting	*Anaphalis* spp.	Summer	All
Phlox	*Phlox* spp.	Summer	All
Asters	Many different genera	Summer–Fall	All
Goldenrods	*Solidago* spp.	Summer–Fall	All
Lupine	*Lupinus* spp.	Early summer	East and Northwest
Joe-pye weed	*Eutrochium purpureum*	Late summer	East
Maryland golden-aster	*Chrysopsis mariana*	Late summer	East
New England aster	*Symphyotrichum novae-angliae*	Late summer	East
Indigo	*Baptisia alba, B. australis*	Spring	Midwest
Prairie verbena	*Glandularia bipinnatifida*	Spring–Fall	Midwest
Prairie smoke	*Geum triflorum*	Early summer	Midwest
Sunflowers	*Helianthus* spp.	Late summer	Midwest
Compassplant	*Silphium laciniatum*	Summer	Midwest
Coneflowers	*Rudbeckia* spp.	Summer	Midwest
Obedient plant	*Physostegia virginiana*	Summer	Midwest
Rocky Mountain bee plant	*Cleome serrulata*	Summer	Midwest
Showy tick-trefoil	*Desmodium canadense*	Summer	Midwest
Bluets	*Houstonia* spp.	Spring–Summer	South
Tickseeds	*Coreopsis* spp.	Summer	South
Coneflowers	*Rudbeckia* spp.	Summer	West
Penstemon	*Penstemon* spp.	Summer	West
Rocky Mountain bee plant	*Cleome serrulata*	Summer	West
Showy tick-trefoil	*Desmodium canadense*	Summer	West
Shrubby cinquefoil	*Dasiphora fruticosa*	Summer	West

FLOWERS

Common Name	Scientific Name	Blooming Season	Region
Tickseeds	Coreopsis spp.	Summer	West
Desert marigold	Baileya multiradiata	Spring–Fall	Northwest
Buckwheat	Eriogonum spp.	Summer	Northwest
Cinquefoil, Potentilla	Potentilla spp.	Summer	Northwest
Desert sand verbena	Abronia villosa	Spring–Summer	Southwest
Indian paintbrushes	Castilleja spp.	Early summer	Southwest
Blanket flowers, Indian blankets	Gaillardia spp.	Summer	Southwest
Purple prairie clover	Dalea purpurea	Summer	Southwest
Rocky Mountain zinnia	Zinnia grandiflora	Summer	Southwest

SHRUBS & TREES

Common Name	Scientific Name	Blooming Season	Region
Cherries, plums, chokecherries	Prunus spp.	Spring	All
Shadbush, juneberry, serviceberry	Amelanchier spp.	Spring	All
Eastern redbud	Cercis canadensis	Spring	East
Spicebush	Lindera benzoin	Spring	East
Blackhaws, nannyberries, arrowwood, and other viburnums	Viburnum prunifolium, V. lentago, V. dentatum, V. spp.	Early summer	East
Buttonbush	Cephalanthus occidentalis	Early summer	East
New Jersey tea	Ceanothus americanus	Early summer	East
Sweet pepperbush	Clethra alnifolia	Summer	East
Madrone	Arbutus arizonica, A. spp.	Spring–Summer	West
Manzanita	Arctostaphylos spp.	Spring–Summer	West
Rose meadowsweet	Spiraea splendens	Summer	West
Salal	Gaultheria shallon	Spring–Summer	Northwest
Buckbrush, whitethorn, wild lilac	Ceanothus spp.	Early summer	Northwest
California buckeye	Aesculus californica	Early summer	Northwest

VINES

Common Name	Scientific Name	Blooming Season	Region
American wisteria	Wisteria frutescens	Spring	East
Carolina jessamine	Gelsemium sempervirens	Spring	South
Trumpet vine	Campsis radicans	Summer	East
Purple passionflower	Passiflora incarnata	Late summer	South

BUTTERFLIES MATTER

Butterflies and moths are more than just a pretty pair of wings. By their sheer volume, they provide much of the fuel and energy that powers their ecosystems, as well as bringing their own appetites to bear on plants to keep them in balance. In the course of her life, a single female butterfly may lay hundreds of eggs. Only two of those eggs need to survive, grow through adulthood, and successfully reproduce to replace their parents and maintain the population. But between hatching and adulthood, those hundreds of individual caterpillars grind away at their host plants, are plucked up by birds to feed their ravenous chicks, are consumed by parasitic wasp larvae, or survive to pupate. After they metamorphose into adults, these butterflies may pollinate hundreds of flowers, feed hungry birds and mammals, or mate to produce the next generation of butterflies.

Unfortunately, butterflies' dependence on specific host-plant relationships, ecosystems, and climates means that they are badly threatened by habitat loss. Land that humans use for agriculture, homes, and commerce is nearly useless for many wild species because of landscaping choices and pesticides. As natural space is developed for human habitat, it is often eliminated as habitat for wildlife.

Over the last several decades, numbers of pollinating insects have plummeted. Some may be familiar with North American monarch butterflies' precarious situation, with about 80 percent of the eastern population lost over the last twenty years due in part to habitat loss and disappearing milkweed. But monarchs are the most visible victims of a trend that threatens thousands of species of insects. Habitat loss is a major factor, but we can't discount how successfully pesticides have worked in agriculture and residential gardening, and how effective herbicides are at eliminating insect-feeding "weeds" in agriculture and highway medians. The consequences are rippling through ecosystems. Both plants and birds lose when pollinators such as butterflies and bees disappear. Unpollinated plants can't produce seed, and birds have more trouble feeding their chicks.

When residential areas incorporate native species in landscaping and we mimic natural habitats in our gardens, the value of those spaces improves drastically for wildlife. Many wild creatures are incredibly adaptable. As long as the conditions are right, some are able to use habitat at close range to humans.

With natural habitat at a premium, every improvement to make human space more butterfly-friendly boosts the resilience of local species to other threats.

Making developed areas more useful to wildlife is only a part of the solution. As you learn more about the lives of butterflies, and learn to love them, you'll grow more invested in the other major element: habitat preservation. Ecosystems are complex and layered, with history and functions that we simply can't replicate in our yards or restorations. The most important thing to do to help butterflies, other pollinators, and the birds, animals, and plants that depend on them is to maintain and protect existing natural habitat so it endures long after we're gone. Habitat preservation is the only way to ensure a future for all the butterflies, making the world a more beautiful place.

Involve Your Kids

Butterflies make fantastic nature ambassadors for kids. Give them an unforgettable experience—and a fun science experiment at home or school—by raising a caterpillar to adulthood!

BUTTERFLIES 101

Keep your butterfly neighbors safe! Don't buy mail-order caterpillars. They come from farm-raised butterflies, may carry diseases, and can also introduce weak or unsuitable genes into your local population when you release them.

You will need food plants for your caterpillars and a roomy container, such as a 10-gallon aquarium tank or a mesh-sided cage. If your yard includes caterpillar host plants, such as those in the species profiles, caterpillars or eggs will be fairly easy to obtain, and you'll have enough food available to satisfy their appetites.

Try not to handle caterpillars or eggs. They're fragile, and some species have hairs or spines that can cause irritation. Snip off the leaf or stem the caterpillar is using, and place the plant in a narrow vase of water to prevent the caterpillar from falling in. Feed the caterpillar leaves from the plant you found it on, most likely its host plant. Clean the cage, replace the food each day, and add some propped-up sticks and twigs to the container so the caterpillar can crawl up and hang to pupate. Most caterpillars will finish growing in a couple of weeks.

Some caterpillars may pupate through the winter. Leave the container in an unheated garage or a shed to keep the butterfly in stasis through the winter. Don't forget to check it in early spring so you can release the butterfly when it emerges.

The chrysalis may change color when the butterfly is ready to emerge. Make sure there's plenty of room for the adult butterfly to stretch its wings. Close quarters easily damage the new, soft wings and will cripple the butterfly for the rest of its life.

If you're lucky, you'll be there to watch the adult butterfly emerge and pump its wings for the first time. Keep a new butterfly no more than a few hours after it emerges. Open the lid to release the butterfly into a blooming garden where it can eat before moving on to search for mates.

Quick ID Tips

These tips will help you quickly recognize the different groups of butterflies:

- Swallowtails have wide, pointed wings and trailing tails.

- Oranges are small and orange or yellow.

- Sulphurs are about 2 to 3 inches across and bright yellow, often with pink edging.

- Whites are small and white, sometimes with black or gray veins.

- Coppers and hairstreaks are tiny and are usually gray with black spots on the underside of their wings. Coppers have a bright, metallic sheen to their upper wings. Hairstreaks usually, but not always, have threadlike tails.

- Blues also have gray underwings with black spots, but males' wings are usually brilliant metallic blue on top.

- Monarchs and other milkweed butterflies are large, with brown or orange wings.

- Fritillaries are brown and orange with black or dark brown dots, dashes, squiggles, and marbling. Greater fritillaries have white or "silver" spots on their underwings.

- Many admirals are mimics of species with toxic defenses, but the shapes of their wings usually differ from the butterflies they imitate.

- Emperors have a triangular shape, with long, pointed forewings.

- Ladies have a cobwebbed, camouflage pattern on their underwings and a distinctive close-winged profile with squared-off forewing tips.

- Tortoiseshells and commas have characteristic jagged edges, squared-off or recurved forewing tips, and small, tail-like points on their hindwings. Their wings are typically bright orange on top, but camouflaged below.

- Satyrs are brown and have eyespots.

- Spread-wing skippers have fat bodies and look more like day-flying moths than skippers.

- Grass skippers perch with their forewings held erect at a forty-five-degree angle, and their hindwings held horizontally, giving them a fighter-jet profile. They're usually tiny and are often colored orange or brown.

Once you recognize which group the butterfly belongs to, note finer details such as color and placement of field marks (eyespots, white bands, and iridescence) to help you identify what you've seen.

PROFILES OF BACKYARD BUTTERFLIES

This section introduces fifty-five of the most common butterflies in North America—from tiny, thumbnail-sized skippers to giant swallowtails and fritillaries. I've included butterflies you're likely to find across large regions of the continent, but keep in mind this is only a small sample of the hundreds of butterflies that live in North America. While all the butterflies on these pages are widespread, some live in more limited ranges and specific habitats, which are described in each profile. Don't worry if you can't yet tell a comma from a cabbage white. Keep reading for plenty of tips on how to recognize, attract, and nurture some of the common butterflies you'll see in your backyard and beyond.

Eastern tiger swallowtails are among the biggest, boldest garden butterflies.

BUTTERFLIES BY REGION

SPECIES	NORTHWEST	SOUTHWEST	TEXAS	MIDWEST	SOUTH	NORTHEAST	WESTERN PROVINCES & ALASKA
Swallowtails							
Pipevine swallowtail (p. 44)			X		X		
Zebra swallowtail (p. 46)				X	X		
Black swallowtail (p. 48)	X		X	X	X	X	
Eastern tiger swallowtail (p. 50)			X	X	X	X	
Western tiger swallowtail (p. 52)	X	X					
Spicebush swallowtail (p. 54)			X	X	X	X	
Giant swallowtail (p. 56)		X	X	X	X		
Oranges and Sulphurs							
Sleepy orange (p. 58)		X	X		X		
Clouded sulphur (p. 60)	X	X	X	X	X	X	X
Southern dogface (p. 62)		X	X	X	X		
Whites							
Checkered white (p. 64)	X	X	X	X	X	X	X
Cabbage white (p. 66)	X	X	X	X	X	X	X
Harvesters							
Harvester (p. 68)			X	X	X	X	
Coppers							
American copper (p. 70)				X		X	X
Purplish copper (p. 72)	X	X		X			X

SPECIES	NORTHWEST	SOUTHWEST	TEXAS	MIDWEST	SOUTH	NORTHEAST	WESTERN PROVINCES & ALASKA
Hairstreaks							
Coral hairstreak (p. 74)	X	X	X	X	X	X	X
Banded hairstreak (p. 76)			X	X	X	X	
Brown elfin (p. 78)	X				X	X	X
Eastern and Western pine elfin (p. 80)	X	X			X	X	X
Gray hairstreak (p. 82)	X	X	X	X	X	X	
Blues							
Eastern and Western tailed-blue (p. 84)	X	X	X	X	X	X	X
Spring azure (p. 86)	X	X	X	X	X	X	X
Snouts							
American snout (p. 88)		X	X	X	X	X	
Monarchs							
Monarch (p. 90)	X	X	X	X	X	X	X
Fritillaries							
Variegated fritillary (p. 92)		X	X	X	X	X	
Meadow fritillary (p. 94)				X		X	X
Great spangled fritillary (p. 96)	X			X		X	X
Aphrodite fritillary (p. 98)				X		X	X

BUTTERFLIES BY REGION (CONTINUED)

SPECIES	NORTHWEST	SOUTHWEST	TEXAS	MIDWEST	SOUTH	NORTHEAST	WESTERN PROVINCES & ALASKA
Admirals							
White admiral and red-spotted purple (p. 100)			X	X	X	X	X
Viceroy (p. 102)	X	X	X	X	X	X	X
Emperors							
Hackberry emperor (p. 104)		X	X	X	X		
Tawny emperor (p. 106)			X	X	X		
Ladies							
American lady (p. 108)		X	X	X	X	X	
Painted lady (p. 110)	X	X	X	X	X	X	X
Red admiral (p. 112)	X	X	X	X	X	X	X
Tortoiseshells and Commas							
Milbert's tortoiseshell (p. 114)	X	X				X	X
Mourning cloak (p. 116)	X	X	X	X	X	X	X
Question mark (p. 118)			X	X	X	X	
Eastern Comma (p. 120)			X	X	X	X	
Buckeyes							
Common buckeye (p. 122)		X	X	X	X	X	
Crescents							
Pearl and Northern crescent (p. 124)	X	X	X	X	X	X	X

SPECIES	NORTHWEST	SOUTHWEST	TEXAS	MIDWEST	SOUTH	NORTHEAST	WESTERN PROVINCES & ALASKA
Satyrs							
Common ringlet (p. 126)	X	X				X	X
Little wood satyr (p. 128)			X	X	X	X	
Common wood-nymph (p. 130)	X	X	X	X	X	X	X
Spread-Wing Skippers							
Silver-spotted skipper (p. 132)	X	X	X	X	X	X	
Northern cloudywing (p. 134)	X	X	X	X	X	X	X
Juvenal's and Horace's duskywings (p. 136)			X	X	X	X	
Common checkered-skipper (p. 138)	X	X	X	X	X	X	X
Grass Skippers							
Least skipper (p. 140)			X	X	X	X	
Peck's skipper (p. 142)	X		X	X	X	X	X
Tawny-edged skipper (p. 144)				X	X	X	
Dun skipper (p. 146)	X		X	X	X	X	
Hobomok skipper (p. 148)				X		X	X
Zabulon skipper (p. 150)			X	X	X		
Delaware skipper (p. 152)			X	X	X	X	

Pipevine Swallowtail

HOW DO I IDENTIFY THEM? Pipevine swallowtails are midsized, dark butterflies whose distinctive markings are a popular color pattern mimicked by several other butterfly species. Adult pipevine swallowtails are distasteful thanks to the caterpillar's diet of toxic pipevines, and mimics attempt to secure some of that defense for themselves by copying the pipevine swallowtail's iridescent blue or blue-green coloration above, and glowing orange spots on the underside of the hindwing. Pipevine swallowtails have a line of small, pale dots arranged along the edge of the hindwing and a row of seven large, round, orange spots around the curve just inside the blue field of the hindwings. The blue on the wings of male pipevine swallowtails is more brilliant than that of females. The black caterpillars have paired rows of orange or red spots down their back, and they wave several pairs of fleshy, antennae-like tentacles overhead.

WHERE DO I FIND THEM? Look for pipevine swallowtails in open woods and forest edges, along creeks and in gardens. They move constantly, fluttering quickly past at waist height and gently pumping their wings when perched at rest. Males often gather at puddles to sip nutrients. They live throughout the southern United States and south through Mexico, though they often spread northward and colonize habitat as far north as New York and Massachusetts.

WHAT CAN I DO TO ATTRACT THEM? Adult pipevine swallowtails feed on nectar, and they favor plants with large, trumpet-shaped flowers. Azaleas, lilacs, phlox, lantana, thistles, and petunias will attract adults to feed in your garden. Caterpillars feed exclusively on pipevine or Dutchman's pipe (plants in the genus *Aristolochia*), storing up the toxins they use to deter predators. Some pipevine plant species are native as far north as New England and the Great Lakes area.

LIFECYCLE Females lay their eggs in clusters, and young caterpillars are often found in groups on their host plants. They disperse as they get older, foraging alone until they pupate. The chrysalis is green and brown, and it is fastened upright to a stem, tied on with a belt of silk around the middle. Adult butterflies emerge in late spring in the northern part of their range and will continue reproducing in several generations through the late summer and into the fall in the South. Pipevine swallowtails may reproduce throughout the entire year in areas that do not freeze in the winter. In colder areas, the butterfly overwinters as a pupa.

AT A GLANCE	
HABITAT:	Open areas; woods and forest edges
PREDOMINANT COLORS:	Black, blue, orange
SEASON MOST OFTEN SEEN:	Spring through summer
MIGRATORY:	No

Zebra Swallowtail

HOW DO I IDENTIFY THEM?   The zebra swallowtail is the only whitish swallowtail in its range, with black stripes streaking its 2½- to 4-inch wings from front to back. The tails are much longer than those of most of our other swallowtails, sweeping back from a cloudy blue patch on the upper side of the hindwings and bright red spots that form a heart where the wings meet. A red bar fills space between stripes on the underside of the hindwing. The bodies of both males and females are also black and white striped. Fine black or green and white stripes arch across the caterpillar's smooth skin, interspersed with electric yellow accents.

WHERE DO I FIND THEM? Zebras live in wet lowlands and damp, deciduous forests, swamps, and riversides. Adults feed in nearby open fields, meadows, and pastures. Their range covers the southeastern United States, from the Great Plains east to the coast and down through Florida. They are rarer in the north, through southern Wisconsin and Michigan and the southern border of Pennsylvania. Zebra swallowtails fly at about head height. Caterpillars are typically found alone; females spread their eggs around singly, and the caterpillars are known to cannibalize each other.

WHAT CAN I DO TO ATTRACT THEM? Adults feed on nectar from a wide variety of plants. They actively feed and mate for most of the year in their southern range and from early spring through summer in their northern range. A full-season floral palette of native plants in their range might include redbud, blueberry, verbena, dogbane, viburnums, and common milkweed. The caterpillars feed exclusively on pawpaws (*Asimina* genus) that typically grow in the understory of deciduous forests.

LIFECYCLE Zebra swallowtails produce two generations in the northern part of their range and multiple generations per year in their southern range. They're active from early spring through the end of the summer in the North and year-round in the South. Males patrol for females on open hilltops and through the understory of forest trees. Caterpillars acquire bitter-tasting compounds from the pawpaws they eat, making them unpalatable to birds, and they also have an *osmeterium*—an orange, forked scent organ they brandish to fend off insect predators. Like many swallowtails, zebra males spend time sipping nutrients from puddles and mud, and they may gather with hundreds of other butterflies at productive puddles. They overwinter in colder zones as hibernating pupae, dangling from the undersides of leaves.

AT A GLANCE	
HABITAT:	Damp forests and open fields
PREDOMINANT COLORS:	White and black
SEASON MOST OFTEN SEEN:	Year-round
MIGRATORY:	No

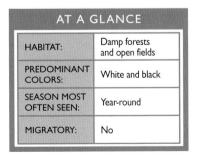

Black Swallowtail

HOW DO I IDENTIFY THEM? The female black swallowtail seems to mimic the toxic pipevine swallowtail with a similar iridescent blue field on the upper hindwing and a splash of red, yellow, and blue spots on the underside of the hindwing. These are small swallowtails, with a wingspan of 3¼ to 4¼ inches. Female black swallowtails have a row of yellow dots edging the forewing above and a cluster of yellow spots at the point of the forewing below. Female black swallowtails also have two messy rows of red spots separated by a blue field on the underside of the hindwing. Males have a yellow band crossing their wings, mirrored by a line of yellow dots. Both sexes have a pair of red eyespots between their tails. Caterpillars start out as small, black, spiky larvae with a white splash, resembling a bird dropping. They grow into large green or white smooth-skinned caterpillars with yellow-spotted black stripes.

WHERE DO I FIND THEM? Black swallowtails are found in nearly every kind of open space, from gardens and parks to open fields, meadows, and roadsides. Their larval food plants grow well in disturbed areas, such as old fields, roadsides, and pastures. They range from southern Canada through Mexico, and they're common east of the Rockies to the East Coast. Adult males puddle along with other swallowtails, sulphurs, and hairstreaks.

WHAT CAN I DO TO ATTRACT THEM? Caterpillars feed on plants in the parsley family. I've often discovered clutches of caterpillars when harvesting dill and parsley from my own garden. The caterpillars will quickly decimate a pot of herbs while they complete their caterpillar stage, and they feed on carrots, celery, and parsnips as well. If you don't want to sacrifice your entire crop, black swallowtails are usually amenable to being hand-raised to adulthood, and they also feed on common wild plants such as Queen Anne's lace. Adults feed on nectar, especially from thistles and milkweed.

LIFECYCLE Gardeners often find lumpy green black swallowtail chrysalises leaning off of nonhost plants without ever having found caterpillars. If you happen to meet the caterpillars, they may treat you to a defensive display in which they inflate an orange, forked organ called an *osmeterium* from behind their heads that emits harmless but nasty-smelling chemicals. Adults are active from spring to fall and produce one or two generations in the North, and three or more in the South. In colder areas, these butterflies overwinter by hibernating in their chrysalises.

AT A GLANCE	
HABITAT:	Open areas
PREDOMINANT COLORS:	Black and yellow
SEASON MOST OFTEN SEEN:	Spring through fall
MIGRATORY:	No

Eastern Tiger Swallowtail

HOW DO I IDENTIFY THEM? Named for their black-and-yellow-striped wings, eastern tiger swallowtails are among the larger butterflies in your garden, with a wingspan between 2½ to 4½ inches. They sail and glide in flight with brief flapping interludes between swoops. Females come in the standard yellow, as well as a black form with shadow stripes. This black color morph may be a way for female eastern tiger swallowtails to disguise themselves as bad-tasting pipevine swallowtails. Females of both color morphs have an iridescent blue patch on their upper hindwings, while males show only a thick black band around the entire wing perimeter. To tell them apart from other yellow swallowtails, look for five wide black stripes, and a blue band and red spots on the underside of the hindwing.

WHERE DO I FIND THEM? On warm summer afternoons, eastern tiger swallowtail butterflies gather in sunlit clearings to court and mate. They chase each other and crowd on flowers to refuel. Tiger swallowtails favor forests, yards, and gardens, and they accumulate in clearings over streams and near rivers. Damp patches of bare ground attract males who seek the salts and minerals found in soil. They are found from Colorado and central Texas east to the Atlantic Coast, and from the Gulf of Mexico north to Minnesota and southern New Hampshire.

WHAT CAN I DO TO ATTRACT THEM? Adults feed on nectar from a wide variety of shrubs and flowers, and since caterpillars also eat the leaves of many different trees and shrubs, yards that include a range of native plants appeal to them. Caterpillars have been known to eat wild cherry, birch, tulip tree, shadbush, and poplar leaves. In spring, adults feed on lilac and wild cherry, as well as other blooming shrubs. Plant milkweed, joe-pye weed, and ironweed to provide nectar later in the summer.

LIFECYCLE Eastern tiger swallowtails are active from February through November in the South and from May through September further north in their range. Caterpillars start life disguised as black-and-white bird droppings, but in later phases they sport a pair of eyespots that resemble a snake face, which may deter predators. They feed high in treetops and wrap a leaf around themselves to hide. Caterpillars from the last brood of the year spend the winter pupating in their chrysalises, suspended from a twig with a single silk thread wrapped around the middle like a belt.

AT A GLANCE	
HABITAT:	Woods, yards, gardens
PREDOMINANT COLORS:	Yellow and black
SEASON MOST OFTEN SEEN:	Summer
MIGRATORY:	No

Western Tiger Swallowtail

HOW DO I IDENTIFY THEM? Though they share a name, eastern and western tiger swallowtails are very different. For instance, westerns do not have separate male and female forms, which eliminates one source of confusion. These are large swallowtails, up to 4 inches across. Western tigers are yellow with black stripes sweeping back from the leading edges of their wings. A wide black band edges their upper wings, and the band draws a nearly perfect vee across open wings. Western tigers have a scattering of small light spots buried in the black band and a pair of red spots between the tails. Below, the black markings thin out. A pale blue band crosses the underside of the hindwing. Another western swallowtail, the two-tailed, can be differentiated from the western tiger by its thinner tiger stripes and a second, short pair of tails. Western tiger caterpillars start out with brown-and-white bird-dropping camouflage and develop yellow eyespots and green skin that resembles the head of a snake.

WHERE DO I FIND THEM?   Western tigers range from the eastern slope of the Rocky Mountains west to the coast and north across the border into British Columbia. They're more common in moist parts of their range than in the dry Southwest. Look for them near streams and rivers, in canyons and oases, but also in residential areas, parks, and roadsides. These butterflies are known for puddling, and where they're common, you might find dozens gathered at a single spot. Males patrol and "pace" along canyons and streamsides in search of females. They are the most common swallowtail in their range.

WHAT CAN I DO TO ATTRACT THEM?   Water-wise native plant landscaping will enhance habitat for all butterflies. Caterpillars feed on leaves from several different trees, including willows, cottonwood, ash, aspen, and *Prunus* species. Adult western tigers feed on nectar. Plant zinnias, California buckeye, thistles, abelia, and yerba santa, as well as milkweeds and butterfly weed, to invite western tiger swallowtails.

LIFECYCLE   Western tigers produce a single generation each year in most of their range. They are active in midsummer at peak bloom. They breed year-round along the Pacific Coast, and there they can produce two or three generations. Caterpillars curl leaves around themselves and tie them together with silk. Like their relatives, these caterpillars possess an orange *osmeterium*—the forked gland that warns predators and emits noxious odors when disturbed. A female can lay up to a hundred eggs on several different host plants. Western tigers overwinter as pupae.

AT A GLANCE	
HABITAT:	Streamsides and canyons
PREDOMINANT COLORS:	Yellow and black
SEASON MOST OFTEN SEEN:	Summer
MIGRATORY:	No

Spicebush Swallowtail

HOW DO I IDENTIFY THEM? Spicebush swallowtails are one of the largest pipevine swallowtail mimics, at 3 to 4 inches across. Spicebush swallowtails are more likely to be confused with female black swallowtails, as they share the same iridescent blue patches (green on the male spicebush) on the hindwing and a similar yellow-and-red spot pattern on the underwing. Spicebush swallowtails have a single row of white spots around the edges of their wings above and a double row of red-and-blue spots below. These spots are often small and gumdrop-shaped rather than round. Spicebush swallowtails are missing a single red spot in the sequence on each hindwing, filling the space with a blue mark that resembles a comet. Young caterpillars use bird-dropping camouflage, but as they grow older they develop a pair of large eyespots on a green background, thought to resemble a snake.

WHERE DO I FIND THEM? Spicebush swallowtails are low, fast fliers. Males gather at puddles in the right habitat, especially where spicebush is found. These butterflies are most often found in forests, fields, roadsides, pine barrens, and swamps throughout the eastern part of the United States, north to Canada, and south through Florida and Texas. They're common and active in their range from April through October and year-round in Florida. They do not often wander northward, so a spicebush swallowtail outside its range is a rare find.

WHAT CAN I DO TO ATTRACT THEM? Adult spicebush swallowtails feed on nectar from a variety of long-throated flowers. Azaleas and sweet pepperbush are attractive native shrubs that grow well in shaded

areas, and these have full, rounded growth that fit well into a more formal garden. Jewelweed is another favorite nectar plant. The caterpillars feed on spicebush and sassafras. Adding either of these plants to your yard will improve the habitat for caterpillars and attract adult butterflies as well.

LIFECYCLE Active for most of the warm season, spicebush swallowtails produce two generations that overlap each year. Spicebush swallowtails are active year-round in Florida. The caterpillars spend daylight in rolled leaves and emerge to feed at night. When they're ready to pupate, they turn yellow or brownish and leave their host plants in search of a good location. These caterpillars are sometimes found quite far from host trees. Some caterpillars from each generation overwinter as pupae, emerging in the spring as adults to court and mate.

AT A GLANCE	
HABITAT:	Forests, roadsides, swamps
PREDOMINANT COLORS:	Black, blue, red
SEASON MOST OFTEN SEEN:	Spring through fall
MIGRATORY:	No

Giant Swallowtail

HOW DO I IDENTIFY THEM? Lots of yellow? Teardrop tails? Enormous? The giant swallowtail and the eastern tiger swallowtail vie for "biggest butterfly" award, but the giant earns points for the flashy pattern crossing its 4- to 6½-inch wings. This swallowtail swaps zebra stripes for a bold yellow cross embedded in the black background of the upper wings. Below, the wings are pale yellow with a light blue stripe crossing the hindwing. Three small red spots accent the blue. The tails are uniquely rimmed with black, enclosing characteristic yellow teardrops. The caterpillar mimics a bird dropping from hatch to pupation, wearing brown and white blotches across its back. Caterpillars display a smelly orange *osmeterium* when they feel threatened.

WHERE DO I FIND THEM? For a butterfly so closely tied to its host plant, citrus, it is surprising that its range stretches as far north as Wisconsin and Michigan, and west through the Great Plains and arid Texas to Southern California. Though less common in the North than in the South, giant swallowtails use several northern plants such as prickly ash and Hercules' club, which in fact belong to the citrus family. They are very common in citrus

groves, where their caterpillars, known as orange dogs, may reach pest-level populations. In their range, seek giant swallowtails on hillsides along rivers, in parks and gardens, and anywhere that citrus grows. Males seek minerals at puddles.

WHAT CAN I DO TO ATTRACT THEM? Caterpillar host plants hoptree (*Ptelea trifoliata*) and northern prickly ash (*Zanthoxylum americanum*) are cultivated for ornamental use and can be planted in northern areas where the giant swallowtail is found. Ornamental and culinary citrus trees are, of course, the plants of choice for those living in the South, though in those areas you may lose your crops to the ravenous caterpillars. You can also plant common rue (*Ruta graveolens*), a nonnative herb, to attract them. The adults feed on nectar, so complement your caterpillar host plants with a flowerbed of nectar-bearing native plants, including goldenrods, milkweeds, and azaleas.

LIFECYCLE Giant swallowtails produce two generations each year in the North, where they are active from May through September, and three or more generations in the South. They breed year-round in Florida. Males patrol appropriate habitats in search of females, bouncing in flight with slow wing flaps that carry them several feet at each stroke. Females lay a single egg on each leaf. Giant swallowtails spend the cold months in diapause as pupae.

AT A GLANCE	
HABITAT:	Orange groves and riversides
PREDOMINANT COLORS:	Yellow and black
SEASON MOST OFTEN SEEN:	Spring through fall
MIGRATORY:	No

Sleepy Orange

HOW DO I IDENTIFY THEM? Dainty sleepy orange butterflies zip around, perching only to busily sip nectar or slurp up minerals from puddles. They are named for a small dash on the upper side of their forewing that resembles a closed, or "sleepy" eye. It's unlikely that you'll see this field mark, though. They nearly always perch with their wings closed, so you're more likely to get a good look at their bright yellow underwings and mottled patch in the middle of the hindwing. The upper side of the wings is bordered in thick black, surrounding an orange or tan-ish patch. Sleepy oranges have a 1½- to 2¼-inch wingspan and perch with their forewings tucked behind their hindwings, collapsing their profile into a shallow triangle. The caterpillars wear a coat of short peach fuzz over their mint-green skin and white side stripes.

WHERE DO I FIND THEM? Sleepy oranges seek out low, open, sunny areas. They live throughout the southern United States and Mexico, north to Missouri and southern Pennsylvania. Like many southern butterflies, they roam in the late summer, spreading farther north than usual. Check puddles and gravel roads. There's likely to be a few sleepy oranges among all the sulphurs, swallowtails, and blues. Males patrol open paths and gullies in search of females.

WHAT CAN I DO TO ATTRACT THEM? Wide, sunny areas within the sleepy orange's range will probably see these butterflies passing through in search of host plants. Adults feed on nectar from a wide variety of plants, preferring plants in the aster family, such as tickseeds and thistles. Caterpillars feed only on pea-family plants, particularly wild senna, but are known to eat cassias, and others, including partridge pea and sensitive plant.

LIFECYCLE Sleepy oranges do not tolerate cold very well and are slightly migratory, contracting their population southward in the fall and returning to the northern edges of their range in late summer. In the heart of their range, these butterflies breed year-round, but further north they manage two to four broods during their breeding season. Females lay a single egg on the underside of a host plant leaf. Pupae are small and green, strangely bulbous in the middle, but pointed at both ends. The pupa is attached at the base to a stem, head up, and leans away from the plant it's attached to. These butterflies overwinter as adults in the northern zones of their range.

AT A GLANCE	
HABITAT:	Low, open areas
PREDOMINANT COLORS:	Yellow and orange
SEASON MOST OFTEN SEEN:	Year-round in range
MIGRATORY:	Yes

Clouded Sulphur

HOW DO I IDENTIFY THEM? Clouded sulphurs are small 1½- to 3-inch yellow butterflies that belong to a family of several similar small, yellow species. Males have dark gray or black edging the upper side of their wings, a small dark dot in the middle of the forewing, and a small reddish-pink dot in the middle of the hindwing. The undersides of the wings are edged in pink or gray. Males have two white spots, sometimes double-ringed, as well as an arc of small dark spots on the hindwing and a larger dark spot on the forewing. Females come in two forms: yellow and white. The dark upper wing edge markings on females are fainter than those of males, and they enclose yellow or white squares on the forewing. Females have spots in similar placement to males. The upper wings are difficult to see, as the butterfly flutters rapidly and perches with wings closed. You can sometimes approach close enough to see the upper wing pattern illuminated by the sun. The small caterpillars are light green with some peach fuzz and yellow stripes along each side.

WHERE DO I FIND THEM? Clouded sulphurs favor open spaces such as pastures, meadows, hayfields, and road edges, where they can be found working over nearly every blooming plant as they travel. Their flight is rapid but weak. Males gather at puddles, sometimes in large accumulations with other species. Their range spreads from Alaska and most of Canada south to Georgia and the middle of Texas, and from the Atlantic Coast westward to the border of California.

WHAT CAN I DO TO ATTRACT THEM? Clouded sulphurs are one of the most common butterflies in their range and habitat, so a sunny, open yard with short, nectar-filled flowers will attract them. They feed on a wide variety of plants, especially thistles, red and white clover, goldenrod, and verbena. Their flight season lasts from late spring through the end of October; design your garden for continuous blooming to encourage visitors. Caterpillars feed on legumes, a diverse family of plants that includes peas, clovers, vetch, and wild indigo.

LIFECYCLE Adults are active from May through October, with a longer flight period further south in their range. They can produce three to five generations in a year, depending on the length of the breeding season. They overwinter as hibernating caterpillars but may also spend the winter in the chrysalis, emerging as adults to feed and seek mates in late spring.

AT A GLANCE	
HABITAT:	Open meadows and marshes
PREDOMINANT COLORS:	Yellow and gray
SEASON MOST OFTEN SEEN:	Summer
MIGRATORY:	No

Southern Dogface

HOW DO I IDENTIFY THEM? The southern dogface is similar to the common and widespread clouded sulphurs, though larger, with a 2¼-inch average wingspan. A closer look at the butterfly at rest reveals its characteristic pointed forewing and the cartoonish poodle's face showing through from the other side of the wing. On the closed-winged butterfly, the wings are edged in pink, and the forewing and hindwing both have bold eyespots in the middle. On the upper side of the wing, the male has a thick black border enclosing the poodle face and a patch of black at the base of the forewing. The female's forewing markings are less well organized and more faded. The caterpillars are smooth and green, with a white and red side stripe and yellow or white stripes crossing over the back.

WHERE DO I FIND THEM? The southern dogface is a resident of Mexico, southern Texas, and Florida, but spreads north each year to become common throughout the Southwest and Midwest during the summer. Alfalfa is the larval host plant, and the air above alfalfa fields is sometimes thick with clouds of dogfaces in flight. They also fly over dry, open fields; shortgrass prairies; roadsides; open woodlands; and washes. Males patrol for females and puddle. They fly swiftly and directly, as if they know exactly where they're headed.

WHAT CAN I DO TO ATTRACT THEM? Alfalfa is both a primary caterpillar host plant and a nectar source for adult southern dogfaces, so if you have a hay meadow and you live in their range, you likely have them already. The caterpillars also feed on other small-leafed legumes, such as false indigo and clovers. Adults feed on nectar from many wildflowers, including pretty plants such as coreopsis, verbenas, and bluets.

LIFECYCLE Southern dogfaces spread northward each year if the conditions are appropriate, colonizing suitable habitat as far north as Illinois and South Dakota. They breed from May through September in their southern range, producing up to three generations. Once the last generation metamorphoses into adults, they suspend reproduction over the winter. This generation spends much of the time conserving energy and perching in the sun on shrubs. They live several months longer than the earlier generations, restarting their reproductive capabilities in the early spring. Dogfaces that spread north produce a single generation or may fail to reproduce at all. The pupae are green, swollen, and round in the middle, looking like a tightly closed flower bud leaning off of a stem.

AT A GLANCE	
HABITAT:	Fields and meadows
PREDOMINANT COLORS:	Yellow, black
SEASON MOST OFTEN SEEN:	Year-round in range
MIGRATORY:	No

Checkered White

HOW DO I IDENTIFY THEM? This small white butterfly belongs to a family full of small white butterflies and can easily be mistaken for others. But the proof is in the checks on their 1½-inch wings. Checkered white females have a distinctive pattern of dark gray markings that trace the veins of their upper wings. The marbling on the underside of their hindwings is variable, ranging in color from yellow-brown to greenish-tan, with darker markings common in the spring. Males are white, with black markings concentrated on the forewing. Their flight is low and swift, and they can be mistaken for cabbage whites in flight. Look for a dark, rectangular marking toward the front of the forewing, compared to the cabbage white's precise dot. Caterpillars have velvety green skin with lengthwise yellow stripes and scattered black speckles.

WHERE DO I FIND THEM? This widespread butterfly is found throughout the continent, though it's absent from New England and rare in the East. They're very common in the West and the South. Checkered whites favor disturbed and open areas, such as vacant lots, pastures, and roadsides, where host plants in the mustard family are often found. They are frequent garden visitors, attracted by nectar plants and cultivated mustards such as cabbages and kale.

WHAT CAN I DO TO ATTRACT THEM? Asters, clovers, and mustards are pioneer plants that often colonize disturbed areas, and these seem to appeal to nectar-feeding adult checkered whites. Caterpillars feed on plants in the brassica family, including cresses, mustards, and cabbages, as well as Rocky Mountain bee plant (*Cleome serrulata*) in the West. In the East, they're known to feed on Virginia and prairie pepperweeds. If you find caterpillars on your veggie-patch cabbages, you might be able to raise them to adulthood on other appropriate food plants, while sparing the majority of your crop.

LIFECYCLE Checkered whites are active as adults from March through November, typically producing three generations during their breeding season. Males patrol for females, often circling hilltops and bare, high places. They visit puddles to seek minerals. Males emerge earlier than females and often outnumber them early in the season. Caterpillars feed on the flowers and fruit of their host plants. Checkered whites overwinter in the chrysalis. Pupae are light blue-green, with some faint striping along the sides. Like other butterflies in this group, checkered white pupae fasten themselves vertically to stems tied with a silk belt to the plant.

AT A GLANCE	
HABITAT:	Open fields and disturbed areas
PREDOMINANT COLORS:	White and black
SEASON MOST OFTEN SEEN:	Spring through fall
MIGRATORY:	No

Cabbage White

HOW DO I IDENTIFY THEM? Cabbage whites may be the easiest butterfly to recognize, as well as the most common. They have unmistakable reverse-domino coloration, with greenish-yellow to white wings, dark bodies, and dark points on the upper side of the forewings. The forewings are marked with black dots—one dot in the middle for males and a pair of dots on females. They fly gracefully from plant to plant as they search for mates. They spend a lot of time on garden plants, thoroughly combing flowers for every last drop of nectar. Cabbage white caterpillars are smooth green, with short velvet fuzz and a yellow stripe on their side.

WHERE DO I FIND THEM? The cabbage white is a European species accidentally introduced in Quebec around 1860. From there, it has expanded its range throughout the United States and Canada. These hardy butterflies appear in gardens, roadside plantings, open fields, cities, agricultural areas, and just about every other kind of habitat except thick forests. They thrive in urban areas and are often the only butterfly encountered in dense downtowns. Cabbage whites are considered a pest species in agricultural areas because of their caterpillars' voracious appetite for plants of the brassica family: mustards, cabbages, kale, and other similar vegetables. The caterpillars bore holes deep into the heads of cabbages or align themselves with the ribs of kale leaves where their camouflage renders them invisible.

WHAT CAN I DO TO ATTRACT THEM? You'll likely see cabbage white butterflies without any extra landscaping effort at all. Adults feed on flower nectar from any available plant, including dandelions and common bedding flowers such as marigolds and chrysanthemums. Vegetable gardens are especially attractive to cabbage whites since they often include favored host plants for caterpillars. Any gardening or wildflower planting done for other butterflies will appeal to cabbage whites as well.

LIFECYCLE Cabbage whites are one of the earliest butterflies to emerge after winter, and they're usually the first butterfly you'll see in the spring in most residential areas. In northern regions, they produce two to eight generations through the breeding season. In the South, they breed year-round. Males patrol for females and bask with wings spread in the sun. Cabbage whites fly until the first hard frost, also making them the last butterfly many people see until spring. They overwinter as angular pupae, which are variably green or brown and speckled or mottled.

AT A GLANCE	
HABITAT:	Open meadows and marshes
PREDOMINANT COLORS:	White and black
SEASON MOST OFTEN SEEN:	Summer
MIGRATORY:	No

Harvester

The harvester could easily be mistaken for a member of the hairstreak group due to its size, 1 to 1¼ inches, and its overall shape and underwing markings, though it lacks the tails of the hairstreaks. North America's only carnivorous butterfly, harvesters are more colorful than the hairstreaks they resemble, with washes of rusty orange, rose, and violet, and brick-colored spots ringed with brighter lavender. When they fly, they flash an orange-and-black pattern on their upper wings that resembles skippers. Caterpillars are hard to spot; they're gray and fuzzy naturally, but they disguise themselves further to blend in among their prey—woolly aphids—by weaving a sheet of silk and sticking the corpses of their prey to their backs like a cloak.

WHERE DO I FIND THEM?   In their range, from the Plains east to the coast, through Texas and north to Canada, harvesters hang out in swamps, along streams, and in deciduous forests where damp vegetation encourages infestations of woolly aphids. Check plants such as alder, ash, beech, and hawthorn for clusters of woolly aphids, which look like clumps of cottony mold, and then look closely for the well-disguised gray caterpillars or their aphid-corpse camouflage. Adults perch high on sunny leaves and dash out to attack other butterflies that pass. Males patrol and return to the same perch repeatedly. Harvester butterflies have unusually short proboscises, so instead of feeding on nectar flowers, they sip aphid honeydew and feed on animal droppings and occasionally carcasses.

WHAT CAN I DO TO ATTRACT THEM?   Planting a sacrificial alder may attract a woolly aphid colony that will eventually catch the attention of passing harvesters, who are known to wander far and wide in search of their prey. However, both the aphids and the harvesters are unpredictable. The best practice is to go where harvesters are most likely to be found—swamps, marshes, and humid forests.

LIFECYCLE   The harvester is fascinating due to its carnivorous diet, but that specialization enables other impressive capabilities. The protein a caterpillar gains from its prey results in one of the shortest cycles from caterpillar to adult—a mere three weeks. Harvesters are active from spring through fall and can produce anywhere from two to six or more generations, depending on prey availability and the length of the season. Their chrysalis is squat and round and has darker markings that are said to resemble a monkey face. They likely overwinter as pupae, but this hasn't been confirmed by observation.

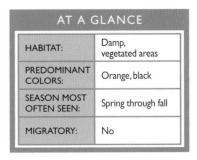

AT A GLANCE	
HABITAT:	Damp, vegetated areas
PREDOMINANT COLORS:	Orange, black
SEASON MOST OFTEN SEEN:	Spring through fall
MIGRATORY:	No

American Copper

HOW DO I IDENTIFY THEM?   Coppers are so-named for the metallic orange patches that flash on their upper wings, and they often pause spread winged to bask on flowers in the sun. American copper butterflies can look like two different species, depending on whether they perch with wings open or closed, but both males and females have similar coloring. The underside of their wings is silvery gray with a bright orange patch on the forewing, delicate black dots, and a jagged orange line edging the hindwing. Above, the bright orange forewing contrasts with the velvety dark gray-brown hindwing, which is edged with a matching orange band. Black dots are scattered all over. They are no more than 1 inch wide.

WHERE DO I FIND THEM?   Though they're called American coppers here, this species is found throughout the world. Like many butterflies, they are most active on warm, sunny afternoons. Look for them in meadows and marshes, roadsides, and other open, disturbed areas. Vacant lots and landfills are often full of plants such as clovers, asters, and sorrels that attract American coppers. Males perch on low flowers or grass to wait for females to pass. They are found throughout the Midwest and Northeast, from Iowa east to Maine, and south to Tennessee and North Carolina. There are also small western populations with duller coloring, found as far north as Alaska.

WHAT CAN I DO TO ATTRACT THEM?   These butterflies prefer weedy, sunny spaces, so letting a patch of your yard go a little wild will encourage them to visit. Caterpillars eat plants in the buckwheat family, especially sheep sorrel and curled dock. Adults nectar on low-growing plants with small flowers, such as clovers, asters, yarrow, hawkweed, thistles, butter and eggs, and butterfly weed. Many of the preferred food plants readily colonize disturbed areas such as driveway and garden bed edges. These butterflies will often let a slow, quiet observer lean close enough to appreciate every tiny spot and wing scale while they feed, as long as you don't let your shadow fall on their wings.

LIFECYCLE   Adults fly during the warm summer months—June through September in the northern part of their range and a little longer further south. Caterpillars are no bigger than ½ inch and are green and sluglike. They breed in two cycles further north. Further south, they may breed three times or more, depending on the climate. American coppers spend the winter pupating in brown chrysalises, low in vegetation or in the leaf litter, emerging in early summer as winged adults.

AT A GLANCE	
HABITAT:	Open meadows and marshes
PREDOMINANT COLORS:	Gray and orange
SEASON MOST OFTEN SEEN:	Summer
MIGRATORY:	No

Purplish Copper

HOW DO I IDENTIFY THEM? This 1½-inch copper is named for the metallic magenta-to-lavender blush of the male's upper wings, overlaid on a ground of brown scales and black spots. An orange band traces the tail edge of the hindwing. The female could be mistaken for a tiny fritillary, with orange wings and a pattern of black dots organized into bands and checks on her upper wings. Purplish coppers of both sexes have dove-gray or orange-blushed underwings speckled with a pattern of black spots and dashes and a broad orange band on the edge of the hindwing. The purplish copper closely resembles another species, the Dorcas copper, which lives in higher altitudes and further north than the purplish copper. Female Dorcas coppers are usually darker and duskier than purplish coppers, but in many cases males can't be told apart. Purplish copper caterpillars are green and flattened, with fine white hairs and yellow or reddish lines from head to tail.

WHERE DO I FIND THEM?

Purplish coppers are common from California east through the Rockies and up into Canada, and they range through the Upper Midwest as far east as Ohio. They are the most common copper in the West but are much rarer in the East, where they are outnumbered by the American copper. Search in open areas, wet meadows, valleys, roadsides, disturbed areas, and along streams. Wet habitats support the moisture-loving host plants of caterpillars. They fly low and bask with wings spread on flowers and low perches. Males perch to display and patrol in search of females.

WHAT CAN I DO TO ATTRACT THEM?

Adults feed on nectar. They prefer flowers with shallow nectaries that they can reach with small tongues, such as cinquefoils, which are both nectar sources and a host plant for the caterpillars. Choose native cinquefoils appropriate to your area to support purplish coppers. Asters, thistles, Queen Anne's lace, and goldenrods make good additions to wildflower beds, though purplish coppers are not often found in gardens. Caterpillars also feed on docks and knotweeds that may occur naturally in wilder areas of your yard.

LIFECYCLE

The reproductive rate of purplish coppers varies more by altitude than by latitude, with up to three generations each year at lower elevations and as few as one generation at the highest elevations. They're active May through September in lower elevations and further south and in July through August at their highest elevation. Females lay eggs at the base of host plants or among the leaf litter underneath. They overwinter in the egg stage.

AT A GLANCE	
HABITAT:	Fields and meadows
PREDOMINANT COLORS:	Orange, gray, purple
SEASON MOST OFTEN SEEN:	Summer
MIGRATORY:	No

Coral Hairstreak

HOW DO I IDENTIFY THEM?   Despite lacking tails altogether, the coral hairstreak is one of the most common, and largest, members of the hairstreak group in its range. Their 1- to 1½-inch wings are brown above; the underside is a light brownish gray, occasionally showing a wash of peach across both wings. A row of orange (coral) spots rims the outside of the hindwing. An interior row of black spots on both wings is usually ringed with white. While many hairstreaks have a characteristic patch of metallic blue scales at the back edge of the hindwing, the coral hairstreak has no blue at all. The caterpillar is green and shaped like a pill bug, with burgundy markings on its tail end and behind the head.

WHERE DO I FIND THEM?   The coral hairstreak is common in the East and as far south as Georgia. It roams to central Canada but is less common further west. The preferred habitat is overgrown open areas, weedy clearings, old pastures, barrens, and other similarly open, dry habitats. Males perch on top of shrubs or patrol above bare hilltops to attract females. Caterpillars hide at the base of their food plants and feed at night. Many hairstreaks, including the coral, engage in fascinating mutual relationships with ants, which defend the caterpillars against predators in return for a sweet liquid secreted by the caterpillar, called honeydew. If you see a cluster of ants on coral hairstreak host plants, look closely for a well-camouflaged caterpillar.

WHAT CAN I DO TO ATTRACT THEM?   Adult coral hairstreaks feed on nectar from plants such as dogbane and New Jersey tea, but favor butterfly weed—the pretty orange-flowered milkweed of open habitats. The caterpillars feed on cherry and plum trees, which can also provide food and habitat for a wide variety of species in addition to coral hairstreaks.

LIFECYCLE   This common butterfly produces only a single generation each year, and so it has a limited time period when it's on the wing as an adult. Coral hairstreaks are most common for a few weeks in the early summer, though they peak later in July and August in the northern part of the range. Caterpillars hatch in the spring, feed and pupate for a few weeks, and emerge as adults. Eggs spend the rest of the summer, fall, and winter in a suspended state, hatching in the following spring to feed on new growth on their host plants.

AT A GLANCE	
HABITAT:	Clearings and weedy openings
PREDOMINANT COLORS:	Orange, gray
SEASON MOST OFTEN SEEN:	Summer
MIGRATORY:	No

Banded Hairstreak

HOW DO I IDENTIFY THEM? Banded hairstreaks, like other hairstreaks, belong to the genus *Satyrium*, which have a similar appearance: closed-winged, triangular posture, gray wings, white and black markings, fine threadlike tails, and an orange eyespot on the trailing edge of their hindwing. The different species are distinguished by the subtleties of their markings. Banded hairstreaks measure only about 1 inch across their spread wings. They have a long pair and a stubby pair of tails on each hindwing. Just in front of the tails, they show a glittery blue patch and an orange eyespot. The blue patch does *not* have an orange cap. It has rows ("bands") of black and white dashes, sometimes paired to create a wider stripe across the wings. The caterpillars are flattened and sluglike and are green, darkening with a rosy tinge as they age.

WHERE DO I FIND THEM? The banded hairstreak is the most common butterfly in this group, so you're likely to find it if you look at the right time. They're found throughout the eastern United States and parts of central Canada, from the edges of the Rockies and the Midwest, east to the coast and down through Florida. They live in forests and are especially visible in sunny clearings or edges. The males wait in trees, darting out to engage other butterflies in whirling skirmishes that spin up into the treetops and out of sight before returning to their perches.

WHAT CAN I DO TO ATTRACT THEM? Banded hairstreak caterpillars feed on native oaks, walnuts, and hickories. They are butterflies of the forest, so they're more likely to use your yard if it's forested, though they're adaptable as long as caterpillar host plants are nearby. If you live near suitable habitat, you can also provide nectar sources, including dogbane, milkweeds, New Jersey tea, and meadowsweet—native plants that will be blooming while the adults are active.

LIFECYCLE These butterflies produce a single generation each year and are usually active for about four weeks in early summer. Caterpillars feed on the catkins of oaks, emerging in early spring before the oak trees leaf out and eating the new, tender leaves as they emerge. Females lay their eggs on the twig ends of the host plant, where the buds are already forming for next year's new growth. The egg will endure, unhatched, through the rest of the summer and the following winter until the next spring.

AT A GLANCE	
HABITAT:	Forests
PREDOMINANT COLORS:	Gray and orange
SEASON MOST OFTEN SEEN:	Early summer
MIGRATORY:	No

Brown Elfin

HOW DO I IDENTIFY THEM?   Though the most common member of the Elfin family, they are rather rarely seen. These tiny brown butterflies are aloft on their 1-inch wings for about a month in earliest spring. Their browns may be rosy, have a purple or green sheen, or be sprinkled with black scales. Certain populations may be lighter and more orange than others. Their fringe—the soft hairy edge of their wings—is usually checkered with black. The caterpillars are small, green, and trilobite-shaped, with a rosy or lighter green scalloped pattern along the back.

WHERE DO I FIND THEM? Brown elfins live in barrens, bogs, boreal scrub- and pine-oak forests—throughout Canada and the West and in the Northeast and South at higher elevations along the spine of the Appalachian Mountains. If you know the *where*, the next important part is the *when*. Brown elfins produce a single generation each year, and the adults are only active for about a month in the early spring, near their bog habitats. Bare soil paths are good opportunities to find brown elfins. They sip moisture from puddles or damp soil. Males perch near host plants to display conspicuously and wait for females passing by. Because they are so small, they are often concentrated in colonies—where you find one, you may find many.

WHAT CAN I DO TO ATTRACT THEM? It is best to be situated in the right habitat to begin with. If you live near pine-oak forest or similar habitats within their range, brown elfin–friendly plants will thrive in the acidic soils that occur there. Caterpillars in the East feed on the flowers and fruits of plants in the heath family, which includes attractive shrubs and border plants such as blueberries, huckleberries, leatherleaf, and Labrador tea, as well as low-growing bearberry. In the West, caterpillars switch to manzanita, madrone, buckbrush, and similar plants. Adult brown elfins feed on nectar. Plants that bloom during their early spring flight period include all the caterpillar hosts mentioned above, as well as spicebush, willow, winter plum, and shadbush in the East.

LIFECYCLE As noted earlier, brown elfins produce a single generation each year. Adults are fairly long-lived for butterflies, lasting more than twenty days. They deposit eggs around the unpredictable weather of early spring and the caterpillars hatch in time to eat the new flowers of their host plants, as well as the resulting fruits through the summer. They drop down to the leaf litter to pupate through the winter.

AT A GLANCE	
HABITAT:	Barrens, pine-oak forests, scrub
PREDOMINANT COLORS:	Brown
SEASON MOST OFTEN SEEN:	Early spring
MIGRATORY:	No

Eastern and Western Pine Elfin

HOW DO I IDENTIFY THEM? These two species are indistinguishable to the casual observer, except for geographic range. Other butterflies resemble the pine elfins, but they are rarer and less widespread. The nickel-sized, handsome brown and black pine elfins don't scare easily. The patterns of brown and black banding are very similar between eastern and western, though the westerns have elongated triangular markings on the rear edge of their hindwings. Easterns may show a metallic frost on their hindwings when they are newly hatched. Their upper wings are dark brown or rusty, but they never show these as they always perch closed-winged. Caterpillars are flattened and shaped like pill bugs, green with yellow stripes from head to tail and covered in short, fine orange or red hairs.

WHERE DO I FIND THEM?   Pine elfins are never far from a pine or pine-oak forest, or pine barrens. Adults feed on nectar so they may roam nearby roadsides, forest edges, or old fields. The eastern lives in boreal forests throughout Canada, dipping down around the Great Lakes, and populating the Northeast and much of the South. Westerns are found in pine forests through the Rockies, Nevada, and California, stretching into Alberta and British Columbia. Pine elfins are absent from the Midwest, Plains, and Texas, due to the lack of appropriate habitat. Search the tops of young pine trees, where males perch to wait for females. Males puddle, and all pine elfins pause on sunny trails to bask in the sun. If you move slowly enough, you may be able to coax one onto your fingertip.

WHAT CAN I DO TO ATTRACT THEM?   Caterpillars feed on native pine trees, such as pitch, white, jack, and scrub in the East, and limber, lodgepole, and ponderosa pines in the West. Adults also require nectar during their brief flight period. Adult easterns fly in earliest spring and feed on blueberries, cinquefoil, shadbush, white sweet clover, and other early blooming native plants. Westerns fly from spring through summer and feed on small-flowered plants, such as succulents, biscuitplant, pussy toes, and everlastings.

LIFECYCLE   Pine elfins may be present as adults for up to three-month spans, starting as early as February in their southern range and April through June in the north. They produce a single generation each year. The caterpillars feed on pine needles and then pupate. Pine elfins spend the winter in their chrysalis and emerge in the spring when nectar sources are available and the pines are sending out fresh growth.

AT A GLANCE	
HABITAT:	Barrens, pine-oak forests, scrub
PREDOMINANT COLORS:	Brown
SEASON MOST OFTEN SEEN:	Early spring
MIGRATORY:	No

Gray Hairstreak

HOW DO I IDENTIFY THEM? The understated, small, but dapper gray hairstreak, a 1½-inch butterfly, is found bouncing through open habitats nationwide. We have several similar hairstreaks, but the gray hairstreak is dark gray above, with red-orange spots on the hindwings just in front of the whiskery tails that give its name. Below, they are an even light gray, with a row of white and black dashes that follow the curves of its wings. A small red splotch with a black dot draws attention to the tails, thought to have evolved as a false-head decoy against birds. In fact, gray hairstreaks are often seen with a triangular gouge out of their hindwings, evidence of an evaded bird attack. Like many caterpillars in the hairstreak family, gray hairstreak caterpillars have a squat, plated appearance, similar to a trilobite. They are tiny, less than 1 inch long, and shaded from cream to pink to blend in with the flowers they feed on.

WHERE DO I FIND THEM? Gray hairstreaks prefer open spaces. Roadsides and old fields with blooming flowers will offer plenty of sightings, but their dainty size and subtle coloration means they're rather inconspicuous. They are common from Southern Canada south to Mexico, and from coast to coast. In gardens, they seem to favor large daisies, and they'll spend a long time sipping nectar from each individual floret in the flat yellow disk.

WHAT CAN I DO TO ATTRACT THEM? Gray hairstreaks are almost guaranteed to visit your sunny garden, as long as you provide plenty of nectar-bearing flowers through the growing season. They prefer plants with small

flowers to accommodate their short tongues. Try including dogbane, milkweed, mints, goldenrod, asters, and clovers in your native plant beds. The caterpillars are even easier to satisfy. Unlike many caterpillars that require very specific host plants, gray hairstreaks are generalists and have been documented feeding on dozens of different plants. You are very likely to find gray hairstreak caterpillars feeding on clovers, mallows, and other plants in your garden.

LIFECYCLE Gray hairstreaks are active and common as adults from May to September in the North and from February to November in the South. This long season means they produce between two and four generations each year. Males perch conspicuously at about chest height, waiting for females, and they chase interlopers of all species—insect, bird, and human. They are thought to mate after dark. The butterflies spend the winter as pupae.

AT A GLANCE

HABITAT:	Sunny, open habitats
PREDOMINANT COLORS:	Gray and black
SEASON MOST OFTEN SEEN:	Spring through fall
MIGRATORY:	No

Eastern and Western Tailed-Blue

HOW DO I IDENTIFY THEM? These two butterflies are so similar in appearance and habits that it makes sense to treat them in the same profile here. Most enthusiasts can easily distinguish the two on geography alone. Tailed-blues are tiny, with a wingspread of less than 1 inch. Their flight is low and bouncy, and they stop often to feed and bask in the sun with their wings spread open. Females of both species have gray upper wings, charcoal on the Eastern and brownish on the Western, though the Western female often shows some blue at the wing bases. Males have brilliant blue upper wings. Easterns have bright orange spots on their hindwings, just in front of the whiskery tails. Westerns have no orange spots.

Below, both species have pale gray wings, with scattered black dashes and dots. The caterpillars grow to about ½ inch and are flattened and green with three red and white stripes from head to tail.

WHERE DO I FIND THEM?   Tailed-blues can be quite common in open habitats of all kinds. The best opportunities for getting close occur on wide sunny trails and roadsides. They pause frequently, and thanks to their small wing stroke, you can keep up until they alight. Once perched, they spread their wings, angling into the sun for warmth. Tailed-blues slowly rub their hindwings together, attracting attention to their false antennae and eyespots. This technique appears to work quite well on birds. Many tailed-blues are often found with their tails missing or beak-shaped chunks out of their hindwings, evidence of a bird attack.

WHAT CAN I DO TO ATTRACT THEM?   Tailed-blues feed on low-growing plants with shallow flowers. Asters, verbenas, cinquefoils, white sweet clover, wild strawberry, and toadflax all fit the bill. Eastern tailed-blue caterpillars feed on the flowers and seeds of legumes, including many common yard weeds, such as clovers, vetch, and wild pea. The caterpillars of Westerns also favor legumes, but they prefer the seeds inside the pods of false lupine (*Thermopsis*), milkvetch (*Astragalus*), and other vetches.

LIFECYCLE   Tailed-blues are on the wing from spring through fall and can produce several generations each year, depending on the climate and habitat. Males patrol near the host plants and sometimes perch conspicuously. You may sometimes find a pair of tiny little blues courting on a daisy, both easily able to fit on the face of the flower. Females lay their eggs on the host plant. The last generation of caterpillars of the year hibernates, pupates in the spring, and emerges within weeks as the year's first adult butterflies.

AT A GLANCE	
HABITAT:	Fields and meadows
PREDOMINANT COLORS:	Gray, blue
SEASON MOST OFTEN SEEN:	Spring, summer, fall
MIGRATORY:	No

Spring Azure

HOW DO I IDENTIFY THEM?   The first butterfly of the season is usually a tiny, salt-and-pepper flutterer passing at ankle height, pausing frequently on the path to soak up the warm sunshine. These little butterflies belong to a group of hard-to-separate species collectively known as the spring azures. Once thought to belong to a single species, they are now thought to make up at least four different species only distinguishable genetically. Spring azure wingspans cover a petite ⅞ to 1⅜ inches. The underside of their wings are white to light gray, sprinkled with faint to heavy spots, dashes, and squiggles. They closely resemble eastern and western tailed-blue butterflies, but lack the orange spot on the hindwing. Males are violet-blue above, with thin black edges on their wings. Females have a wide black band tipping the forewing surrounding light blue or white patches and a toothed pattern on the trailing edge of their hindwings. Caterpillars are small, green, and sluglike.

WHERE DO I FIND THEM?   Spring azure butterflies tolerate a wide range of climates, and they live throughout the entire continent, from Alaska to Mexico, though not Florida. Favored habitats include forests and gardens, old fields and pastures, freshwater wetlands, and swamps. Look for them on wide, sunny paths in the earliest part of their flight season. Males are often spotted with other puddling butterflies.

WHAT CAN I DO TO ATTRACT THEM?   Adults feed on nectar from flowers. Fill your yard with small-flowered native shrubs such as viburnums and New Jersey tea in the East. Other native plants, such as dogbane, common milkweed, blackberry, and others with small, clustered flowers, attract dozens of butterflies. Caterpillars feed on the flowers and fruits of several kinds of woody shrubs, including dogwood, New Jersey tea, meadowsweet (*Spiraea alba*), and Collinsia. Leaving your wildflower or border beds alone during your fall cleanup will protect overwintering spring azures while they spend the cold months in diapause.

LIFECYCLE   Spring azures and their relatives start life tended to like royalty by crowds of ants. The caterpillars secrete a sweet liquid called honeydew, which attracts the ants, which may protect the caterpillar from predators in return. Adult spring azures are active from January to October in the southern regions of their range and from May to August at their northernmost limit in Canada. Spring azures can produce several broods through the year. When the weather turns too cold, they spend the winter as pupae in their chrysalises.

AT A GLANCE	
HABITAT:	Open meadows and marshes
PREDOMINANT COLORS:	Gray and orange
SEASON MOST OFTEN SEEN:	Summer
MIGRATORY:	No

American Snout

HOW DO I IDENTIFY THEM? This strange little butterfly, between 1½ and 2 inches wide, looks like it's grown a long, pointy nose like a character from a children's movie. In fact, the fuzzy mouthparts, or palps, of the American snout have evolved to stretch out beyond its eyes, making its leaflike disguise even more convincing. They rarely perch with their wings open, but when they do, you'll see an orange forewing bordered with a black band and white checkers gathered at the point of their squared-off wing tips. American snouts hold their forewings swept back, an unusual posture for butterflies. At rest, their orange and black forewings are usually hidden behind their subtly camouflaged hindwings, which vary from plain to mottled gray. The 1-inch caterpillars are green with yellow side stripes.

WHERE DO I FIND THEM?

Snouts hang upside down from branches, stretching their antennae and palps to resemble leaf stems. They are very hard to spot at rest, but if you see one in flight, you can watch it perch and transform from butterfly to vegetation. American snouts visit mud puddles, but they are skittish and hard to approach. Their low,

zigzag flight is reminiscent of satyr butterflies, but their flashing orange wings will help you tell the difference. Seek them along streams and in moist woods, where their host plants, hackberries, are known to occur. Snouts are most common in the South, especially in Texas and Arizona, but spread north through Illinois and Pennsylvania, and sometimes even further. They're known for heavy migrations, which can fill the skies in Texas on their way north.

WHAT CAN I DO TO ATTRACT THEM?

Caterpillars feed on the young, tender leaves of hackberry plants—trees that make lovely specimen plants for yards and attract other species of butterflies and moths. Nectar-bearing native plants, such as asters, dogwood, dogbane, and sweet pepperbush, feed and attract adults. Later in the season, goldenrods, milkweed, and joe-pye weed will continue to support American snouts at the end of the summer.

LIFECYCLE

American snouts are active May through August in most of their range and produce two generations each year. Males fly low, patrolling back and forth for females in suitable habitat. The chrysalises are green and cone-shaped and hang from leaves and stems. As noted earlier, these butterflies are migratory. They move south in the fall to spend the winters as adults.

AT A GLANCE	
HABITAT:	Moist forests and streamsides
PREDOMINANT COLORS:	Gray and orange
SEASON MOST OFTEN SEEN:	Summer
MIGRATORY:	Yes

Monarch

HOW DO I IDENTIFY THEM?   The monarch may be the most familiar butterfly in North America due to its famous migration, amenity to hand-raising, and, unfortunately, its recent population decline. The orange and black pattern differs between sexes: males are brighter orange, with thin black veins and a raised black dot in the middle of the hindwing. (The dot is a scent organ that produces pheromones to attract females.) Females are browner, with wider black veins. The wings of both sexes are bordered with a wide black band sprinkled with three rows of white dots. Monarch caterpillars are nearly as well known as the adults. They are fat, white larvae with fine yellow and black stripes and a pair of fleshy black feelers behind the head and another on the rear end.

WHERE DO I FIND THEM?   Open habitats where common milkweed grows are the easiest places to find monarchs, but they fly far and wide. News of their

plight has sparked widespread planting of milkweeds, the sole food for caterpillars. In fields where milkweed grows densely, you may find dozens of adults and hundreds of caterpillars crawling all over the plants. Fall migration sends the North American population streaming south, especially along the coasts. On an ocean beach in September, you may see hundreds zipping by, sometimes inches above the waves. Monarchs live in most of Canada, throughout the United States, and in Mexico.

WHAT CAN I DO TO ATTRACT THEM?   Monarchs have become the poster child for insect pollinator decline. Anything you do to help monarch butterflies will also help hundreds of other pollinators. Adults feed on nectar from asters, thistles, milkweed, goldenrod, and many other flowers. To attract monarchs, plant local milkweed species in large clumps.

LIFECYCLE   Until 1975, the winter home of monarchs was only known to people living in the Oyamel Mountains in Central Mexico. That January, an American scientist witnessed butterflies carpeting the trees by the millions, spending the cold months in diapause. The butterflies leave in the spring, breeding and spreading north over three generations. The fourth generation, which hatches at the northernmost edge of its range in late August, heads south without breeding. This generation is one of the longest-lived adult butterflies in North America, surviving as long as ten months to make a 1,000-mile journey, resting through the winter, waking in the spring to return north. The caterpillars grow quickly and, once ready, leave their milkweed host plants, climb another tall plant nearby, and hang in mint green chrysalises speckled with golden dots until ready to emerge as adults.

AT A GLANCE	
HABITAT:	Open, sunny spaces
PREDOMINANT COLORS:	Black and orange
SEASON MOST OFTEN SEEN:	Spring through fall
MIGRATORY:	Yes

Variegated Fritillary

HOW DO I IDENTIFY THEM?   This 2-inch tawny butterfly looks like an orange-tinted relative of the lady butterflies when it perches with its wings closed, thanks to its crescent-shaped profile and cobwebbed hindwing. Above, it has a wide band of pale orange or tan that separates the darker inside half of the wings from the black-dotted orange wing border. The veins and edges are sharply trimmed in black. A pair of light crescents outlined in black are placed on the curved leading edge of the forewing. The forewings are long and pointed, not rounded like other fritillaries, and they lack silver underwing spots. Instead, the underside of the forewing has a distinct light spot circled in black, located just inside the leading edge of the wing. Caterpillars are orange or red with white head-to-tail stripes and black spines.

WHERE DO I FIND THEM? Variegated fritillaries live throughout the South and Southwest and north through Oklahoma and the Great Lakes region. They spread further north in good years, crossing into Canada and roaming into New England. They are grassland butterflies, preferring open spaces such as barrens, disturbed areas, fields, roadsides, meadows, and scrub. Though they remain common, grasslands are one of our most at-risk habitat types, which may affect variegated fritillaries in the long run. They are flighty and hard to approach.

WHAT CAN I DO TO ATTRACT THEM? Caterpillars feed on the seedpods, leaves, and flowers of several garden ornamentals, including passion flower, violets, and pansies. These plants also support the adults who live on nectar. Adults feed on common and swamp milkweed, butterfly weed, mints, sunflowers, and a host of other native grassland flowers. They are active from April through October in the North and year-round in their southern range. Dedicating a section of your lawn to a prairie or meadow attracts them, and they will roam beyond their typical habitat in search of host plants.

LIFECYCLE Variegated fritillaries differ from the greater fritillaries in their life cycle as well as their appearance. Variegated fritillaries produce several generations in most of their range—as many as four in the South where they are year-round residents, though they may produce only a single generation in northern regions. In areas where they do not reproduce year-round, they spend the winter as adults. They do not seem to tolerate extreme cold; experts believe variegated fritillaries head south in the winter to avoid low northern temperatures.

AT A GLANCE	
HABITAT:	Grasslands
PREDOMINANT COLORS:	Orange, tawny brown, black
SEASON MOST OFTEN SEEN:	Spring through fall
MIGRATORY:	Yes

Meadow Fritillary

HOW DO I IDENTIFY THEM?   The meadow fritillary is a 1½- to 2-inch butterfly that is fairly common in its range. They vary from bright orange to dull brown, with a dapper pattern of tidy black checks and spots on the upper wings. The tip of the forewing is just barely squared off, enough to be a distinguishing feature when the butterfly perches with its wings closed. Unlike many fritillaries, the underside of its wings lack any white or silver markings, instead featuring a mottled orange and black pattern on the forewing and a more muted marbled pattern on the hindwing, glazed with violet. The caterpillars are dark, with a row of rear-pointing vees down their backs. They bristle with branched spines all over.

WHERE DO I FIND THEM?   These are butterflies of fields and pastures, meadows, and disturbed areas, though they are spreading to new areas and learning to use similar open habitats as preferred habitats disappear. Meadow fritillaries are present throughout Canada and New England, the Upper Midwest, down

through the Appalachians, and down the spine of the Rockies into Colorado. They're active throughout the summer. Fields where they are present are likely to also host other species of nectar-loving butterflies, so search out the orange butterflies preferentially visiting flowers in the aster family, such as black-eyed Susans, dandelions, and daisies. Males patrol for females, swooping low above the vegetation and occasionally pausing at mud puddles to sip minerals.

WHAT CAN I DO TO ATTRACT THEM?   Plant abundant clumps of flowers from the aster family among your native plant beds. Black-eyed Susans and purple coneflowers (where they are native), New England aster, white wood aster, fleabanes, tickseeds, and coreopsis will do the trick. Like all fritillaries, caterpillars feed on violets. Take care to not disturb areas where violets grow, especially during fall cleanup, since meadow fritillaries overwinter as caterpillars near or on their violet hosts.

LIFECYCLE   Meadow fritillaries follow a more typical reproduction cycle than the greaters, producing two or three generations each year, with adults on the wing throughout the summer. Meadow fritillaries lay their eggs near the host plants, and the caterpillars, upon hatching, have to find the correct plant to feed on by themselves. The chrysalis is a plain, brown spiky case that hangs, head down, from leaves and stems. Meadow fritillaries overwinter as late-instar caterpillars. They pupate in early spring, emerging as adults in time to lay their eggs on young, tender leaves.

AT A GLANCE	
HABITAT:	Fields and meadows
PREDOMINANT COLORS:	Orange, black, lavender
SEASON MOST OFTEN SEEN:	Summer
MIGRATORY:	No

Great Spangled Fritillary

HOW DO I IDENTIFY THEM? This large orange butterfly shares habitat with a better-known orange butterfly, the monarch. But great spangleds stand apart, thanks to their marbled black upper wing pattern and the silver spangles on the underside of the hindwing. Females show darker "shoulders" than the males, whose tawny wings may be dull and tattered later in the season. The underside of the hindwing has a brown patch toward the base of the wing and a buffy band along the outside edge. In western populations, males are bright orange and females have dark brown wings surrounded by pale yellow. The caterpillars are black, with branched red spines from head to tail.

WHERE DO I FIND THEM? Meadows and pastures, fields, roadsides, open forests, and other moist, sunny habitats are often full of great spangled fritillaries in their flight season. They're found from the Pacific Northwest through the Northeast, though not in the Deep South. Large colonies of milkweed in meadows and fields sometimes host hundreds of adults. The caterpillars feed on plants in the violet family, and they also grow in large colonies. Search out patches of violets to see if you can spot the caterpillars sleeping during the day.

WHAT CAN I DO TO ATTRACT THEM? If your yard includes a patch of violets, let them grow instead of mowing them down. They'll spread into a thick, green carpet with purple flowers that will provide nectar for several insect species and food for fritillary caterpillars. Adult great spangled fritillaries have been observed feeding on many native plants: milkweed, joe-pye weed, thistles, verbena, bergamot, and red clover. Include these in formal flowerbeds or wild border beds, or seed part of your yard to grow a butterfly meadow.

LIFECYCLE These butterflies have an interesting and unusual life cycle. Great spangled fritillaries only produce a single generation each year. Males emerge as adults much earlier in the year than females, usually in late spring. Females emerge weeks later. After mating season ends, the males die off. Females continue feeding and then lay their eggs in the late summer. Instead of laying eggs on host plants, however, they lay their eggs near violets on the ground or on other material. The caterpillars hatch, crawl to the nearest violets, and then burrow in among the dead leaves to immediately start hibernating without eating a single bite. These new caterpillars spend the winter with empty stomachs, emerging in the spring along with the new violet growth to eat heavily, pupate, and begin the cycle all over again.

AT A GLANCE	
HABITAT:	Sunny, open habitats
PREDOMINANT COLORS:	Orange, black, and silver
SEASON MOST OFTEN SEEN:	Spring through fall
MIGRATORY:	No

Aphrodite Fritillary

HOW DO I IDENTIFY THEM? The Aphrodite fritillary is so similar in size and coloration to the great spangled that they can be very difficult to separate, especially since they share much of their range and use the same habitats. The Aphrodite has the same sort of marbled black upper wing pattern seen on most of the greater fritillaries. One field mark is a small black dot on the upper forewing, close to the wing base, though it may be obscured by dark scales on some butterflies. The great spangled does not have this marking. Below, the Aphrodite has large white spots on the hindwing. Eastern Aphrodites sometimes have a darker, chocolatey patch that gradually fades into a lighter area toward the wing edge, unlike the more distinct light band of the great spangled. Their forewings are usually redder toward the base with a darker tip underneath the black and white markings. Western Aphrodites have lighter underwings and may even appear as buffy as great spangleds. Caterpillars are dark brown or black, with light-colored spines.

WHERE DO I FIND THEM? Aphrodites use much of the same habitat as great spangleds, including meadows, fields, and pastures, but also use acidic habitats such as barrens, bogs, and open woods. In areas where both are active, great spangleds greatly outnumber Aphrodites. Their range includes most of Canada, the Great Plains and the Great Lakes, the Appalachians down to Tennessee, and up through New England and Nova Scotia.

WHAT CAN I DO TO ATTRACT THEM?   Like most greater fritillaries, Aphrodites depend on violets as their caterpillar host plant. Nurture patches of native violets that occur in your yard. Adult Aphrodites especially love common milkweed and butterfly weed, but they also feed on other summer-blooming wildflowers such as dogbane, joe-pye weed, ironweed, thistles, and goldenrod.

LIFECYCLE   Aphrodites produce a single generation each year, with a reproductive cycle very similar to that of great spangleds. Males emerge up to three weeks earlier than females and start patrolling for mates well before females are available. Females live longer than males, which die soon after the brief mating season ends. They lay eggs near, but not on, host plants toward the end of the summer. Caterpillars hatch but do not feed. Instead they go into hibernation and pass the winter at the base of their future food plants. When spring thaws and the violets begin growing, the caterpillars are within reach of new, tender leaves to feed on.

AT A GLANCE	
HABITAT:	Open, sunny habitats
PREDOMINANT COLORS:	Orange, tawny brown, black
SEASON MOST OFTEN SEEN:	Summer
MIGRATORY:	No

White Admiral and Red-Spotted Purple

HOW DO I IDENTIFY THEM?   Though they look very different, the white admiral and red-spotted purple belong to the same species, a fact recently confirmed with genetic sequencing. The white admiral form is dark, with a wide white band that cuts across the wings. Above, the hindwings are marked with a band of red and blue spots. Below, the butterfly may show more red, including a cluster of black-rimmed red spots between the white band and the base of the wings. Red-spotted purples mimic the pipevine swallowtail, with iridescent blue or blue-green scales on both sides of the wings instead of the white band of the white admiral. Below, the hindwings of red-spotted purples have a row of red spots around the edge, much like the bright hindwing markings of the pipevine swallowtail. They also have black-rimmed red spots close to the body in the same area as the white admiral. Caterpillars of both forms are smooth, mottled brown and green with a light or whitish saddle marking and resemble bird droppings. Their backs are bumpy, and they brandish a pair of branched horns behind their heads.

WHERE DO I FIND THEM?   These butterflies primarily live in forests, both deciduous and evergreen. Both forms spend time basking in the sun on dirt paths and gravel roads. The ranges of the two forms are adjacent to each other, and there's a small band of overlap where they breed together and hybridize. White admirals live further north, concentrated in Canada and New England. Their range is smaller than that of the red-spotted purple. Red-spotted purples can be found throughout the Midwest, east to the coast, and from Wisconsin and New York south to Texas and Florida.

WHAT CAN I DO TO ATTRACT THEM?   These butterflies don't feed on nectar. Instead, they seek out sap flows, rotting fruit, carrion, and dung. Place bananas or oranges on a plate or in a hanging suet cage to attract adults. The caterpillars are known to feed on many different trees and shrubs, including willow, aspen, birch, wild cherry, oaks, and shadbush. Yards with many trees and understory shrubs will better mimic the woodlands they prefer.

LIFECYCLE   White admirals and red-spotted purples are active April through October, usually completing two generations over the course of the breeding season. Males perch on shrubs or bushes about 3 feet off the ground to wait for females to pass by. Both forms overwinter as hibernating larvae or as pupae in their chrysalises, which are also disguised as bird droppings.

AT A GLANCE	
HABITAT:	Woodlands
PREDOMINANT COLORS:	Blue and red or black and white
SEASON MOST OFTEN SEEN:	Summer
MIGRATORY:	No

Viceroy

HOW DO I IDENTIFY THEM? Take a closer look at that petite "monarch butterfly" flying by and you may discover you're actually looking at a very interesting mimic, the viceroy. Viceroys are related to the red-spotted purple and white admiral. Throughout most of their range, the viceroy is bright orange or rusty brown, each wing cell separated by wide black veins reminiscent of the monarch. In the Southwest where monarchs are rarer, the viceroy is brown, with thinner black veins, and a line of white dots across the hindwing, similar to the monarch's relative, the queen butterfly. Viceroys are smaller than both monarchs and queens, with a 3-inch wingspan. The telltale field mark is a narrow black band that cuts through the middle of the hindwing. In flight, viceroys alternate flapping and gliding with wings held horizontally, compared to the monarch's strong flapping and vee-winged sailing. Viceroy caterpillars disguise themselves as bird droppings, either black and brown or green with a white splash across their backs.

WHERE DO I FIND THEM? Viceroys prefer wet habitats such as streamsides, moist forest edges, meadows, and freshwater marshes where their caterpillar host plant, willow, grows thickly. Male viceroys display from perches on shrubs where they can spot females passing by. Their range spans nearly the entire continent, except most of the West Coast and parts of Nevada and Arizona. Adult viceroys feed on nectar as well as carrion, aphid honeydew, and animal dung, so don't be surprised if you happen to find this lovely butterfly in a rather unlovely situation.

WHAT CAN I DO TO ATTRACT THEM? Plant asters, goldenrod, thistles, and joe-pye weed in your native plant beds. To host caterpillars, plant willow in dense thickets that mimic the edge habitats viceroys prefer, and you may even attract adult males to desirable display perches.

LIFECYCLE Naturalists once thought that the viceroy's coloration was meant to protect it from predators familiar with the monarch's bitter taste.

Recently, scientists have discovered that the viceroy produces its own toxins, and now researchers believe that the viceroy's mimicry is an amplification of the protective effect rather than a fake-out. The more bad-tasting orange-and-black butterflies birds encounter, the more likely they are to avoid them altogether. Viceroys are active from May through September in most of their range and year-round in Florida, producing two to three generations. Late-instar caterpillars roll themselves up in a leaf tip bound with silk to spend the winter in hibernation.

AT A GLANCE	
HABITAT:	Moist forests and streamsides
PREDOMINANT COLORS:	Black and orange
SEASON MOST OFTEN SEEN:	Summer
MIGRATORY:	No

Hackberry Emperor

HOW DO I IDENTIFY THEM? Hackberry emperors have a strongly triangular shape with an approximately 1½- to 2½-inch wingspan. The ground color of their upper wings may be warm and rusty or rich brown, with white spangles on the tip of the forewing and a row of black eyespots running from front to back. A crisp zigzag line curves along the back of the hindwing. The pattern on the underwing mirrors that of the upper wing in a muted palette, except for the eyespots, which are ringed with yellow and may include some iridescence in the "pupil." Hackberry emperor caterpillars grow to a little over an inch long and are tapered off at both ends. They're green, with longitudinal white stripes and pointed horns that stretch their face into a triceratops-like mask.

WHERE DO I FIND THEM? The hackberries for which this butterfly is named are so adaptable that you can find hackberry emperors in many surprising locations throughout their range. Due to their versatility and appealing growth habit, hackberries have been planted as urban trees, in parkland, and for landscaping. Whence go the trees, there go the butterflies, from the Southwest, up through Wisconsin, and throughout the East and South, except in New England. Adult males have a reputation for being very territorial, known for flying out from their perches to batter intruders of all species and returning to the same perch. They are attracted to the color white, and like the taste of human sweat, so they may even land on you to get to know you better.

WHAT CAN I DO TO ATTRACT THEM? Adult hackberry emperors feed on sap, scat, and rotten fruit, but caterpillars feed on the young growth of hackberry trees. Hackberries in your yard will be claimed by hackberry emperor males or other hackberry-loving butterflies, such as American snouts or tawny emperors. You can tempt hackberry emperors down out of the leaves by doing a little strenuous yardwork nearby—they may land on you to sip your mineral-rich sweat.

LIFECYCLE Females lay eggs in clusters, and caterpillars live, feed, and overwinter communally, huddled in dead, rolled leaves tied together with silk. In spring, the caterpillars feed on fresh leaves and pupate. The chrysalises are green, round, and tapered on both ends, with light lines that resemble the veins of leaves. Hackberry emperors produce two generations each year and are active from May through October.

AT A GLANCE

HABITAT:	Moist forests
PREDOMINANT COLORS:	Brown and white
SEASON MOST OFTEN SEEN:	Summer
MIGRATORY:	No

Tawny Emperor

HOW DO I IDENTIFY THEM? Tawny and hackberry emperors are another pair of butterflies that seem as if they should belong to the same species, but certain biological habits and markings separate the two. The slightly larger tawny emperors are more orange above. The tips of their forewings are orange or dusky, never black like the hackberry's. Unlike the hackberry, the tawny never has pure white markings—its lightest spots may be pale yellow or orange. The upper hindwing of the tawny may be gray, black, or orange with a row of dark brown or black dots along the rear edge of the wing. Below, the tawny has no eyespots on its forewing; the eyespots on its hindwing are reduced and may have no black "pupils" at all. The caterpillar is green with yellow zigzag stripes and has a flattened head with two spiky horns that, in later stages, make it appear to be wearing a dragon mask.

WHERE DO I FIND THEM?

Tawny emperors appear nearly everywhere that hackberries do, from Texas and across the entire southeastern United States, north to the Dakotas and east to New England. They feed on the same host plant and share much of the same habitat as hackberry emperors. Seek them in woods, near streams and rivers, and even in urban areas and parks, since the hackberry trees they feed on are often used as landscaping plants. These butterflies are territorial and aggressive. Males perch in trees to display for females. They will also investigate passing humans and may perch on your face or arms to sip sweat.

WHAT CAN I DO TO ATTRACT THEM?

As with the hackberry emperor, tawny caterpillars feed on hackberry trees. Adult tawny emperors do not feed on nectar, instead preferring rotting fruit, animal dung, and tree sap. Tawnies also investigate passing humans to sip sweat. You may get a closer look than you expected if one lands on you!

LIFECYCLE

Tawny emperors produce one to three generations each year, fewer in the northern areas of their range than in the southern areas. Females lay large piles of eggs under leaves or on the bark, depositing two hundred to five hundred eggs at a time. The caterpillars live communally, eating leaves down to the ribs and following silk roads laid down by other caterpillars to their next meal. The last generation of the season overwinters as late-stage caterpillars, rolling up a dead leaf and tying it with silk to spend the winter hibernating as a group.

AT A GLANCE	
HABITAT:	Moist forests
PREDOMINANT COLORS:	Orange and brown
SEASON MOST OFTEN SEEN:	Summer
MIGRATORY:	No

American Lady

HOW DO I IDENTIFY THEM?   The lady butterflies include several species of medium-sized butterflies, all around 2 inches wide, that sport a similar eye-tangling cobweb pattern on their mottled brown underwings and colorful upper wings featuring a combination of orange and pink. How to tell them apart? Count the eyespots. American ladies have two large eyespots on the underside of their hindwings. They also have a bright pink patch on the underside of their forewing. Above, the American lady is primarily orange, yellow, and brown, with white spots sprinkled on the black tips of their forewings. One distinguishing feature on the upper wing is a small white dot in the orange patch just below the black forewing tips. This white spot shows through to the underwing as well.

They are fast fliers, darting erratically from flower to flower, but they often perch on flowers with their wings spread open. The caterpillars are vertically striped black and yellow, with red and yellow spots on the black bands. They bristle with black, branching spines.

WHERE DO I FIND THEM?   Any open, sunny natural space is likely to host American lady butterflies, especially disturbed spaces such as pastures and roadsides. Also look for these swift, skittish butterflies in meadows, old fields, and on roadsides and trails where flowering plants are plentiful. Plants with clusters of small flowers, such as viburnum and Queen Anne's lace, keep them busy long enough for good looks. They live across the continent and spread up into Canada in the middle of the summer. Males often patrol hilltops or bare patches where low vegetation makes them especially visible to females.

WHAT CAN I DO TO ATTRACT THEM?   Fill your yard with flowering shrubs and mid-height flowering native plants that bloom from spring through late summer, and you're guaranteed to host American ladies. For caterpillars, plant sunflowers, pearly everlasting, pussy toes, and other plants in the aster family. They are active from spring through the summer and may migrate through your area in the fall. Plant late-season flowers such as asters and goldenrods so American ladies can fuel up as they pass through.

LIFECYCLE   American ladies are active from May through November. Adults fly south in late fall, sometimes in significant numbers. Some butterflies may be hardy enough to survive milder northern winters, and they may overwinter

in parts of the United States, though it's generally believed that American ladies do not tolerate cold weather. Caterpillars tie leaves together with silk to make a nest that they occupy singly.

AT A GLANCE	
HABITAT:	Open meadows and fields
PREDOMINANT COLORS:	Orange and pink
SEASON MOST OFTEN SEEN:	Spring, summer, fall
MIGRATORY:	Yes

Painted Lady

HOW DO I IDENTIFY THEM? The painted lady is marked with a cobwebbed pattern on the brown and gray underside of its hindwing, similar to the American lady, but plenty of details set these two butterflies apart. Painted ladies have a chain of four small eyespots on the underside of their hindwing, and they wear a wash of sunset colors, including orange, pink, and peach, on the underside of their forewing. Above, painted ladies are brown at their wing bases, with a bright patch of orange and yellow on both forewings and hindwings, with dark brown marbling throughout. Their forewings are black tipped and white speckled. They are usually around 2½ inches across. Caterpillar coloration can vary from green to lavender to black, with yellow vertical stripes separating the segments. Branched black spines bristle all around.

WHERE DO I FIND THEM?   Painted ladies are found on every continent except Australia and Antarctica. They don't tolerate cold winters though, so autumn's chill sends North American populations of these butterflies south to Texas and Mexico until spring. Habitat-wise, painted ladies are found almost everywhere, from forests to dunes to roadsides, but especially in open spaces such as meadows, fields, and gardens where plenty of blooming flowers provide ample nectar. Males perch and patrol in bright, sunny areas where females are likely to pass.

WHAT CAN I DO TO ATTRACT THEM?   A yard planted with tall flowering plants, especially thistles and asters, will capture the attention of painted ladies. In fact, painted ladies are sometimes known as thistle butterflies in honor of their affinity for this plant. Caterpillars feed on a wide variety of host plants, including asters, mallows, and legumes, but are known to prefer thistles like the adult butterflies.

LIFECYCLE   Adults are active from May through October in the northern part of their range and breed from October through April in their winter range in southern Texas and Mexico. Females lay a single egg on the chosen host plant. When the caterpillar hatches, it makes a silk nest at the top of the plant, where it can grow and feed safely. Once they've matured, caterpillars hang from plant stems and twigs to pupate in their brown, spiky chrysalises. Adults breed perpetually throughout their seasonal migration. They never really stop moving or reproducing, flowing north and south through the continent as they follow the changing seasons. In some years, their spring migration includes millions of attention-grabbing butterflies pouring northward to repopulate the United States and Canada.

AT A GLANCE

HABITAT:	Open fields, meadows, forests
PREDOMINANT COLORS:	Orange and pink
SEASON MOST OFTEN SEEN:	Summer
MIGRATORY:	Yes

Red Admiral

HOW DO I IDENTIFY THEM? Some believe this butterfly's name is a corrupted version of red admirable, a well-earned moniker for this flashy woodland butterfly, though their markings also call to mind military epaulettes. A red-orange stripe cuts across their brown forewings, white spots speckle their black wingtips, and a bright orange band rims the hindwing. Like other lady butterflies, they have a mottled brown background on the underside of the hindwing and a very ladylike pink patch accented by a splash of violet or blue on the forewing. Red admirals are 2 to 2½ inches across. They fly quickly and often land head down on tree trunks and branches, vanishing when they close their camouflaged wings. Caterpillars come in many different colors, though darker hues are more typical, with black and white branched spines and vertical white stripes between each segment.

WHERE DO I FIND THEM? Red admirals provide a splash of color as they dart through clearings in moist woods, yards, swamps, and wetlands. They live on every continent except Antarctica and Australia, and on many islands throughout the world. Males defend territories and may even attempt to drive away hikers, though if you hold still the butterfly may perch on you.

WHAT CAN I DO TO ATTRACT THEM? Adults prefer fermented fruit and flowing tree sap to nectar. Place a tray of cut overripe fruit in a sunny part of your yard or alternately hang the fruit in a wire-cage suet feeder. They visit flowers as a second choice. It never hurts to include plants such as milkweed, red clover, and asters, as well as shrubs such as buttonbush and viburnums in your garden beds. Caterpillars live and feed on nettles, so let some of your yard grow wild and tolerate plants such as stinging nettle (from a distance) to improve your chances of attracting egg-laying females.

LIFECYCLE Red admirals spend winter in warm southern areas as adults and return to the northern parts of their range in the early spring to begin repopulating their habitats. They are thought to be more cold tolerant than other lady butterflies, and they may overwinter further north than the painted and American ladies. Red admirals may even hibernate as adults in North America, though that hasn't been confirmed. They are active from March through October. Like the other lady caterpillars, these make a nest by wrapping a leaf around themselves and tying it with silk. Caterpillars relocate from their host plant to hang from another nearby stem or plant to pupate.

AT A GLANCE	
HABITAT:	Moist forests and fields
PREDOMINANT COLORS:	Red-orange and black
SEASON MOST OFTEN SEEN:	Spring, summer, fall
MIGRATORY:	Yes

Milbert's Tortoiseshell

HOW DO I IDENTIFY THEM? When perched closed-winged, the well-disguised Milbert's tortoiseshell disappears into its habitat. Fortunately for us, this small, 2-inch butterfly often basks open-winged, disclosing its stunning flame-edged upper wings. Milbert's tortoiseshells are related to the commas and question marks, demonstrated by the tortoiseshell's squared-off forewing and leaflike camouflage. The jagged wing edges break up the butterfly's profile so it blends better with the leaves and bark it hides in. The underwings are divided between a dark patch close to the body and a distinctly lighter brown band on the outside. Freshly emerged butterflies may have lavender frosting over the underside of the wing and a delicate row of lavender spots along the edges of the hindwings. The upper wings have a wide orange and yellow band separating inner black patches from the blue-spotted black rim and a pair of orange "cat eyes" on the leading edges. Caterpillars are black with branched spines and a spattering of white and orange-ish speckles.

WHERE DO I FIND THEM?   Tortoiseshells live in nearly all of the western states, up through Canada and Alaska, and spread across the upper Midwest into the Northeast. They breed in damp habitats such as forests, meadows, and marshes. In the southern parts of their range, they stick to higher altitudes, especially in the Appalachian Mountains. They occasionally roam through residential areas, gardens, and urban parks as far south as West Virginia. Tortoiseshells sip at mud puddles and on animal dung.

WHAT CAN I DO TO ATTRACT THEM?   Adults feed on nectar from thistles and goldenrods. Caterpillars feed on nettles—not usually a welcome garden plant unless you eat the nutritious cooked foliage. But if your yard is large or a little wild, pay attention to any nettles that occur naturally to see if they are used by caterpillars.

LIFECYCLE   Females lay piles of eggs on the leaves of their host plants—researchers have documented up to nine hundred eggs in a deposit—and the caterpillars start their lives feeding in communal silk nests. The caterpillars devour their host plant to the stems and then move on to colonize a new nettle. As they grow, they fan out on their own, living in folded nettle leaves until the time comes to pupate. The pupae are spikey and green-brown, with a metallic golden sheen and hang upside down. Tortoiseshells produce two generations each year, with adults flying in early spring and late summer. They overwinter as adults, using their camouflage to hide out of the elements until spring.

AT A GLANCE	
HABITAT:	Damp areas near boreal forests
PREDOMINANT COLORS:	Black and orange
SEASON MOST OFTEN SEEN:	Spring and late summer
MIGRATORY:	No

Mourning Cloak

Mourning cloak butterflies are especially conspicuous when they first appear in early spring: a large dark butterfly sailing down open trails and between bare trees. They pause to bask often, wings spread on the warm soil of sunny trails. Their 3½-inch wings are chocolatey purple above, edged with a band of yellow that can fade to white over the course of this butterfly's long life. The yellow band encloses a row of iridescent blue dots, and the hindwings end in a pair of very short tails. The underwings are darkly camouflaged with a light border that helps the butterfly blend in to tree crevices. The spiky black caterpillars are speckled with white, and a row of red spots runs down the back between their spines.

WHERE DO I FIND THEM? These butterflies range across the entire continent, from Alaska and Newfoundland to northern Mexico, but are absent from Florida. They roam and migrate, but are most often seen in forests, wetlands, and along roadsides. Mourning cloaks are one of the first large butterflies to appear in the spring and one of the last to be active in the fall.

WHAT CAN I DO TO ATTRACT THEM? Adults feed on sap, especially from oak trees, nectar from early blooming trees, and rotting fruit. They may come to fruit set out on a plate along with other sap-and-fruit eaters. Caterpillars feed on tree leaves and have been found eating willow, cottonwood, elm, birch, and hackberry. Check any native trees that grow in your yard for their communal silk-web nests.

LIFECYCLE Mourning cloaks spend more time as adults than most butterflies—up to ten months compared to a few weeks for many other species—and they produce a single generation each year. They overwinter as adults, creeping into sheltered crevices to hibernate through the cold months, emerging early in the spring to mate. Females lay clusters of eggs on new, tender tree growth, and then die. The caterpillars hatch and build a silk nest they share as they feed and grow. They only spend a brief time as caterpillars, and, after pupating for

another few weeks, they emerge in early summer as adults again. The year's new adults fly and feed for only a short time before they settle into another period of dormancy, called *estivation*, that lets them pass through the heat of summer without drying out. They wake again in the fall, to feed until the time comes for them to crawl into hiding for winter hibernation.

AT A GLANCE	
HABITAT:	Everywhere
PREDOMINANT COLORS:	Brown and yellow
SEASON MOST OFTEN SEEN:	Spring and fall
MIGRATORY:	Yes

Question Mark

HOW DO I IDENTIFY THEM? Even though it's the largest member of the group, the question mark is very much like its relative, the comma. The question mark for which this butterfly is named is even buried on its camouflaged underwing, so before you can see that, you have to spot the leaflike butterfly when it's nearly invisible. Question marks occasionally bask with their wings open, so you can admire their orange wings, long tails, and lavender edges. They have two forms, a summer or early-season form with dark hindwings above and a winter form with glowing orange hindwings. The undersides of the wings vary from shades of textured brown and gray to a lovely lavender. Caterpillars are black with white speckles and yellow or orange stripes from head to tail. They're armored with branched spines covering their entire back.

WHERE DO I FIND THEM? In the eastern part of the United States and extreme southern Canada, question marks are seasonally common in open deciduous forests, especially along streams. They have two separate flight periods, one in the spring and one in late summer and early fall. Males often spend the morning basking in the sun, warming up for the day's patrol. If you have time to pause on a spring hike, hang out in a sunny clearing and watch for question mark butterflies passing through.

WHAT CAN I DO TO ATTRACT THEM? Lots of woodland butterflies, including question marks, feed on sap, fermenting fruit, and animal dung. This means that you're more likely to have question marks in your yard if your property is wooded, as opposed to lush beds of flowers and shrubs. They may also visit if you cut open some soft fruit and leave it in a sunny spot in your yard. You can invite question marks by providing their caterpillar host plants, elms, and hackberries, as well as nettles.

LIFECYCLE Question marks follow a similar life cycle to the commas. The adult winter form butterflies overwinter by hiding in sheltered crevices in trees or in the ground. Some migrate south. They wake up in the spring to live for a few weeks, mate, and produce the year's first generation of caterpillars. These feed, pupate, and emerge in May or June as summer form adults. The caterpillars they produce feed and pupate through the summer and then emerge in autumn as the next generation of winter form adults who will hibernate through the cold season.

AT A GLANCE	
HABITAT:	Woodlands and streamsides
PREDOMINANT COLORS:	Orange, black, lavender
SEASON MOST OFTEN SEEN:	Spring and fall
MIGRATORY:	Yes

Eastern Comma

HOW DO I IDENTIFY THEM? Eastern commas often perch with their jagged wings closed, the lavender-and-brown mottled underwing pattern disguising it as a leaf or tree bark. From this side, the comma's silver "comma" is visible in the middle of the butterfly's hindwing. Commas occasionally bask in the sunshine, showing off their rusty orange upper wings. A pattern of black splotches spreads across the orange field on the forewing. This butterfly comes in two forms: a summer form with dark hindwings and a winter form with lighter brown hindwings marked with dark and gold splotches and dashes. The corners of the hindwings stretch into stubby tails, longer on the winter form and frosted violet on freshly emerged butterflies. The spiny caterpillar is highly variable, appearing in white, brown, black, and reddish forms.

WHERE DO I FIND THEM?

Eastern commas are found east of the Rockies to the East Coast, barely crossing the border into Canada. They're absent in Florida. There are a handful of very similar comma species that occur west of the Rockies, distinguished from the eastern comma by geography

and lighter coloration. Eastern commas favor moist woods, especially close to creeks, rivers, swamps, and marshes. They fly quickly, but they can sometimes be carefully approached when they bask in patches of sunlight on boulders and bright paths. Commas found away from their preferred habitat are likely fall migrants, heading south to hibernate through the winter.

WHAT CAN I DO TO ATTRACT THEM?

Adults do not eat nectar, instead preferring sap, fermenting fruit, and animal dung, an adaptation comon among forest-dwelling butterflies. This is another butterfly that might be attracted to cut-up fruit placed conspicuously in your yard. Caterpillar host plants include nettles, hops, and elms.

LIFECYCLE

Eastern commas produce two generations each year. The summer-form butterflies start as eggs laid in early spring that hatch and feed on young, tender leaves until they pupate. They emerge as adults in May and fly through September. Eggs laid by summer-form adults hatch in the late summer, feed, pupate, and metamorphose into winter-form butterflies in late fall. Winter-form commas are active as adults for a few weeks after they emerge. As the days shorten, they settle into their winter shelters—cracks in trees or in the earth—to hibernate until the next spring. Caterpillars only feed at night, spending daytime wrapped up in leaf edges they tie together with silk for safety. The hanging pupae look like curled brown leaves with a cluster of metallic spots on one side.

AT A GLANCE	
HABITAT:	Wet forests and riparian areas
PREDOMINANT COLORS:	Orange and black
SEASON MOST OFTEN SEEN:	Spring, summer, fall
MIGRATORY:	Yes

Common Buckeye

HOW DO I IDENTIFY THEM?   Common buckeyes bear four namesake yellow-ringed "eyes" on each side, set into darker gray-brown wings. Above, a white band crosses the corner of each forewing. An orange band traces the edge of the hindwings, and a pair of outlined orange bars, like equals signs, adorn each forewing. Spring buckeyes have a sandier background color below with a forewing that matches the pattern of the upper side of the wings in a more muted palette; late-season butterflies are both more boldly and brightly colored, with rosier hindwings than in the spring. In southern Florida, the common buckeye shares habitat with two very similar relatives, the tropical buckeye and the mangrove buckeye. The caterpillar is black, with a finely etched black-and-white diamond pattern, branched spines, and bright red eyes.

WHERE DO I FIND THEM?   This butterfly is a year-round resident in the South from coast to coast and migrates northward in the warmer months, sometimes spreading as far as Canada. Look for common buckeyes in open spaces, such as pastures, roadsides, and old fields. They prefer sunny areas with patches of bare earth, where males like to wait for females to pass. These skittish butterflies are hard to approach, even though they fly low and perch temptingly on the ground. A pair of close-focusing binoculars or a camera with a zoom lens will ease some of the frustration of trying to get close enough to admire a buckeye.

WHAT CAN I DO TO ATTRACT THEM?   The larval food sources of common buckeyes include plants that grow easily in disturbed spaces. These host plants, including members of the plantain family, verbenas, figwort, snapdragons, and toadflax, often show up alongside gravel driveways and dirt roads. Adults feed on nectar, especially from composites such as asters, chicory, and tickseed, and thistles and dogbane.

LIFECYCLE   Common buckeyes reside year-round in the southern range of their habitat, where they reproduce continually instead of in discrete generations. This means they are present in steady concentrations throughout the year in the appropriate habitats. Spring sends common buckeyes migrating north into the far reaches of their range, where they produce two to four generations each year before the adults return to the South for the winter. Caterpillars occupy host plants singly and pupate hanging head down from leaves and stems. The pupae are mottled brown with a light band, squat and thick, with paired light-colored knobs running down the back side.

AT A GLANCE	
HABITAT:	Sunny habitats with low vegetation
PREDOMINANT COLORS:	Orange and brown
SEASON MOST OFTEN SEEN:	Year-round/summer
MIGRATORY:	Yes

Pearl and Northern Crescent

HOW DO I IDENTIFY THEM?   These two dainty orange and black butterflies are so similar that even seasoned butterfly watchers may have trouble separating them in the field where their ranges intersect, so they're treated here in the same account. Crescents are thumbnail-sized scraps of orange that bounce along at ankle height in just about every sunny habitat in North America. Their patterns vary, but the northern typically has more orange on its hindwing above and less black marbling than the pearl. Below, both butterflies have a subtle orange and brown mottled pattern that reminds me of old-fashioned maps. On the underside of the hindwing, the pearl crescent usually, but not always, shows the pearly crescent shape for which it's named, carved out of the mottled orange ground color. Caterpillars are black, with brushy spines along the entire back.

WHERE DO I FIND THEM? These butterflies are active all summer long in open, sunny habitats, from roadsides to pastures to open woods. Northerns seem to prefer moister habitats than pearls, but both are so abundant you're almost guaranteed so see one or the other. They stop frequently to bask in the sun or feed slowly on a flower, gently pumping their wings. The ranges of these two species barely overlap, and you can often tell which one you're seeing based on your geographical location. Northerns live throughout Canada, Maine, and Alaska, dipping down through the Rockies and along the ridge of the Appalachian Mountains. Pearls fill the continent east of the Rockies, through the East and South, down through Texas and into Mexico.

WHAT CAN I DO TO ATTRACT THEM? Crescents particularly like asters, both as larval food plants and as nectar sources. Plant heath, smooth, and bushy asters, and fleabanes and calico aster for blooms that last into late summer. Fill your flowerbeds with plants such as white clover, milkweeds, Queen Anne's lace, and goldenrod for flowers from June through October.

LIFECYCLE Crescents produce several generations through their active season, from April through November in the North, and throughout the year further south. Females lay a stack of eggs sometimes twenty layers deep on a host plant. When the caterpillars hatch, they form a colony that concentrates its strength in great numbers meant to outlast the appetite of most predators. The pupae resemble curled green or brown leaves hanging from plant stems. Adult males patrol back and forth along paths and forest edges in search of females and display from perches on short plants. Crescents overwinter as hibernating late-stage caterpillars.

AT A GLANCE

HABITAT:	Sunny open habitats
PREDOMINANT COLORS:	Orange and black
SEASON MOST OFTEN SEEN:	Spring through fall
MIGRATORY:	No

Common Ringlet

HOW DO I IDENTIFY THEM?　Common ringlets are more colorful than most other satyrs, but the variety of hues can be confusing. The common feature linking the different colorations of this 1½-inch butterfly is a delta-shaped splash of white that crosses the middle of the hindwing. The splash may extend from edge to edge, or it may be faint or colored. The underside of the wings is generally a fine gray, varying in tone from orangish to very green. Their hindwings are darker toward the base inside the white splash. In most populations, the forewings are orange except for gray wing points. Some, but not all, individuals have a yellow-ringed eyespot on the forewing. They rarely show their upper wings, though you may catch glimpses of pale orange or creamy white patches while the butterfly is in flight. The caterpillars are green or brown, with yellow stripes running from the head to their forked tail.

WHERE DO I FIND THEM? Common ringlets live in the North and at higher altitudes, but they have been extending their range further south in eastern North America. They're present in New England, most of Canada, Alaska, around the northern shores of the Great Lakes, and in most of the western United States. They favor grassy habitats, including prairies, lawns, roadsides, fields, and pastures. In the West, they live in mountain meadows, but the cooler temperatures of higher altitudes can suppress butterfly activity. Males patrol just above the vegetation.

WHAT CAN I DO TO ATTRACT THEM? Caterpillars feed on grasses and rushes. Substitute native grasses for the commonly available ornamental grasses, or convert some of your yard to short-grass prairie by seeding with native grasses and flowering plants and letting it grow wild. Adults feed on nectar, unlike most members of the satyr group. Asters, tickseed, clovers, Queen Anne's lace, yarrow, milkweed, and other plants bloom throughout the summer. You can provide winter shelter for ringlets by letting the grasses and other natural material in your plant beds build up into nice thick thatch for caterpillars to nestle in.

LIFECYCLE Common ringlets produce two overlapping broods each year, but they grow very slowly due to the climate restrictions of their northern range. Members of the first generation overwinter as late-instar caterpillars after feeding and growing through the summer, while members of the second generation overwinter as early-instar caterpillars, going into hibernation shortly after hatching in late summer. Chrysalises are green with dark streaks over the wing area.

AT A GLANCE	
HABITAT:	Grasslands
PREDOMINANT COLORS:	Orange and gray
SEASON MOST OFTEN SEEN:	Summer
MIGRATORY:	No

Little Wood Satyr

HOW DO I IDENTIFY THEM? Small, nondescript butterflies bouncing past your ankles during your early summer hike are likely to belong to the satyr family, and little wood satyrs are one of the most common members of this group. Males patrol forest paths and streams, bobbing close to the ground and shying away as you approach. They bask in the leaf litter, where their drab coloring helps them blend in. Little wood satyrs are plain gray-brown, with a 1½-inch wingspan. Above, they have four small eyespots on the corners of their wings. Below, the eyespots are larger and ringed with yellow; a diagonal rusty stripe or paired brown lines cross both fore- and hindwings. They share habitat with other small satyr butterflies, so be sure to look closely at the eyespots of the butterfly in question. Caterpillars are small and drably mottled in brown with a darker stripe down the back.

WHERE DO I FIND THEM?   Little wood satyrs live in open forests, forest edges, and old orchards. Wide paths and grassy areas in parks and forested properties will give you the best sightings. They are found from the Great Plains and the Midwest to the East Coast, and from Florida north to Newfoundland. They can be extremely abundant in the right habitats. Look closely at shrubs along creeks, as these are prime displaying perches for males.

WHAT CAN I DO TO ATTRACT THEM?   Satyrs do not eat flower nectar as a primary food source. Instead, they seek out tree sap and, surprisingly, a sweet liquid called honeydew secreted by aphids, tiny insects that cluster in groups to feed on sap from their host plant. Wood satyrs are more likely to visit wooded properties than gardens. Caterpillars feed on orchard grass (*Dactylis glomerata*) and centipede grass (*Eremochloa ophiuroides*), so let native grasses grow longer in wooded areas. Protect any overwintering little wood satyrs by leaving the year's fallen leaves where they land. The accumulated leaf litter will protect and insulate caterpillars through the winter.

LIFECYCLE   Little wood satyrs are commonly seen flying as adults in late spring and early summer. They usually produce one to three generations each year, depending on the latitude. Populations further north have fewer generations due to the shorter length of the warm season. Little wood satyrs spend the winter as caterpillars, completing the cycle of pupation and metamorphosis after the spring thaw.

AT A GLANCE	
HABITAT:	Open woodlands and forest edges
PREDOMINANT COLORS:	Gray-brown and yellow
SEASON MOST OFTEN SEEN:	Late spring/summer
MIGRATORY:	No

Common Wood-Nymph

HOW DO I IDENTIFY THEM? This large brown butterfly flits weakly through the vegetation, flashing its orange forewing patch and abruptly diving down to disappear among the flowers. Though they're subtly marked, they're worthy of admiration. In most of their range, the distinguishing mark is the pale orange patches on the tips of their forewings, each enclosing a pair of large, black eyespots. The upper side of their wings is an even, dark chocolate brown, though they usually perch closed-winged. Their underwings are a soft gray brown with even black ripples that enhance their camouflage. Wood-nymphs sport a variable number of small eyespots on the hindwings. In the North and West, they lack the orange patch, so you'll need to rely on their size and habitat to separate them from other similar plain satyrs. Their caterpillars are smooth and green, with yellow stripes running from their head to their double-pointed tail.

WHERE DO I FIND THEM? Common wood-nymphs are found across the continent, in every state and throughout Canada. They prefer open habitats such as fields, marshes, prairies, roadsides, and near quiet sunny streams. They're easy to spot from a distance as they travel in circuits around their territories, flying bouncily just above the vegetation. A careful search with binoculars or a camera with a zoom lens will sometimes reveal them, perching motionless under the leaves.

WHAT CAN I DO TO ATTRACT THEM? Caterpillars feed on grasses, including purpletop (*Tridens flavus*), a common grass of the East. Short of letting your yard grow into a wild meadow, you can use native ornamental grasses in your landscape and include plants such as thistles and goldenrod. Adults also feed on rotting fruit, so you may be able to entice them to visit with fruit placed in sunny areas in your yard. In the fall, leave dead vegetation standing to shelter overwintering caterpillars.

LIFECYCLE Common wood-nymphs stagger their emergence as adults, with males appearing earlier than females, a strategy similar to that of the greater fritillaries. Common wood-nymphs produce a single generation each year. Males emerge in May or June, females about a week later. After a brief mating period, males die. Females live through the rest of the summer but may go into dormancy to pass the heat of the season. They deposit their eggs on host plants in late summer. Caterpillars hatch shortly after and immediately go into hibernation without eating. They wake in early spring, eat, pupate, and begin the cycle again in early summer.

AT A GLANCE	
HABITAT:	Sunny, open spaces
PREDOMINANT COLORS:	Brown and orange
SEASON MOST OFTEN SEEN:	Early and late summer
MIGRATORY:	No

Silver-Spotted Skipper

HOW DO I IDENTIFY THEM? Big, dark, and bouncy, the silver-spotted skipper is the largest skipper you'll find in most of its range, and its closed-winged perching posture confusingly makes it resemble a typical butterfly more than a skipper. Its long, pointed forewings, large head, and thick body place it squarely at home among the skippers. They rarely travel far without stopping to nectar on low-growing plants, showing off a large, white hindwing splash—the "silver spot" for which it's named—and orange or bronze forewing bars. The upper side of the wings is dark brown, aside from the forewing bars, which are actually scaleless, translucent areas that you can see right through. Caterpillars have bulgy black eyes and a "neck" where the green, finely striped body tapers off behind the head.

WHERE DO I FIND THEM?   The silver-spotted skipper is perhaps the most common spread-winged skipper in its range, which covers the entire Lower 48 except some areas of the Rocky Mountains and West Texas, crosses the southern border of Canada, and spills into Mexico. They prefer open, sunny spaces and are found in brushy disturbed areas, weedy old fields, roadsides, pastures, and clearings. Watch for a speedy, dark butterfly flying low from plant to plant. Males stake out sunny territories where they perch conspicuously, darting out to chase off intruders.

WHAT CAN I DO TO ATTRACT THEM?   Silver-spotteds are frequent garden visitors. They're said to avoid yellow flowers, so plant native flowers such as buttonbush, milkweeds, thistles, and verbena, as well as zinnias, purple coneflower, and clovers. Caterpillars feed on woody plants in the pea family, especially locust trees, and have also been found on hog peanut, wisteria, and false indigo. If you choose wisteria, be sure to choose the native species, *Wisteria frutescens*; imported wisteria can be highly invasive.

LIFECYCLE   Silver-spotted skipper caterpillars cut flaps into leaves to pull over themselves to hide during the day. To keep their shelters clean and to avoid detection by predators, they fling their frass (feces) away from the nest. Caterpillars emerge to feed at night. Silver-spotteds are among the earliest skippers to emerge and are active from early spring through the fall. They are abundant from May through September in the North, producing two generations each year, and from February through December in the South, where they produce up to four broods. They spend the winter as pupae sheltered inside their leaf nest.

AT A GLANCE	
HABITAT:	Sunny, open habitats
PREDOMINANT COLORS:	Brown and white
SEASON MOST OFTEN SEEN:	Spring through fall
MIGRATORY:	No

Northern Cloudywing

HOW DO I IDENTIFY THEM? The northern cloudywing belongs to a group of plain, brown spread-winged skippers who bear such a close resemblance to each other that it's difficult to separate them in the field. The primary field marks are the arrangement of the small spots on the upper forewing and other tiny markings. The northern cloudywing is the most abundant representative of the group, however, and getting familiar with this common species will help enthusiasts eventually learn to tell the cloudywings apart. Northerns have a scattering of faint light specks on the forewing, which do not line up (unlike the southern cloudywing, which is common in the East and South, with large, hourglass-shaped spots that line up across the forewings). Below, the wings are mottled and may be frosted toward the edges. They perch and feed with their wings spread open, making them look like moths—look for threadlike antennae to prove they're butterflies. Caterpillars are smooth and green and have the typical big-headed proportions of skipper larvae.

WHERE DO I FIND THEM? Cloudywings are found from Canada to Mexico, but they are absent in the deserts of Nevada and Idaho and less common in California and the Northwest. They prefer dry habitats such as scrubby fields, disturbed areas, roadsides, savannas, and dry mountain forests. They are not very skittish, so you may be able to get close enough for good looks at their markings. Males perch low in their territories and bask on bare ground in the sun.

WHAT CAN I DO TO ATTRACT THEM? Caterpillars feed on plants in the legume family, and due to their wide range, they have been recorded feeding on many different plants, including indigo, tick-trefoils, hog peanut, clovers, and other pea relatives. Adults feed on nectar, preferring blue, pink, and white flowers such as verbenas, crown vetch (a naturalized invasive species), dogbane, common milkweed, and clovers. Many butterflies thrive on what we consider to be weeds, though, so letting a bit of your yard grow wild in your flowerbeds will provide nectar for several species.

LIFECYCLE Cloudywings are active in early summer—May through July—in the North where they produce a single generation each year. In the South, they are active from spring through the fall, and they can produce two to three generations in the season. Caterpillars live alone, and they make shelters out of rolled leaves. They pupate in leaf nests tied together with silk. Cloudywings overwinter as a mature caterpillar and pupate in the spring.

AT A GLANCE	
HABITAT:	Sunny, open habitats
PREDOMINANT COLORS:	Brown and white
SEASON MOST OFTEN SEEN:	Summer in the North, spring – fall elsewhere
MIGRATORY:	No

Juvenal's and Horace's Duskywings

HOW DO I IDENTIFY THEM? Duskywings are another group of skippers with very similar coloration and markings. They are dark brown, with subtle, mothlike scalloped and marbled patterns on the upper side of their wings. They vary by size, geographic distribution, larval food plants, and small field marks. Juvenal's and Horace's duskywings are the largest, most widespread and common species of the group. In both species, females have brighter, more distinct patterns above, looking a bit like rich brown Persian rugs. Males are darker but may show some faint patterning. Both species have about a 1½-inch wingspread and perch with their wings open. They emerge in early spring, but Juvenal's only have one generation each year, and they are done flying by early July in the North. Later summer duskywings are most likely Horace's.

WHERE DO I FIND THEM? Juvenal's and Horace's duskywings live throughout the eastern United States. Horace's spreads further west into the Great Plains, and Juvenal's live further north in New England and into Canada around the Great Lakes. They superficially resemble the cloudywings but can be separated by habitat. Duskywings favor open woodlands, forest edges, roadsides, swamps, and oak barrens. Duskywing males perch on the ends of twigs and fly out to display for females. Juvenal's use high perches, and Horace's usually perch close to the ground. In the evening, duskywings wrap their wings flat around a twig, making them appear more mothlike than ever and disguising them for safety through the night.

WHAT CAN I DO TO ATTRACT THEM? These duskywings both feed on oaks as caterpillars. Adults feed on nectar from shrubs and short plants. They are active in early spring and depend on early-blooming plants, such as dandelion, blueberry, redbud, viburnum, and buttonbush. Horace's duskywing is also active through August and makes use of summer bloomers, such as milkweed, goldenrod, mints, and verbenas. These skippers overwinter in leaf litter, so be reserved with fall cleanup to leave their shelter intact.

LIFECYCLE Juvenal's duskywing produces a single generation each year in the North and East, and its active period lasts a few months in the spring and summer, sometimes as early as February in the South. Horace's duskywing produces two generations in the North, where it's active from April through August, and as many as three generations in the South, from January through October. Like many skippers, the caterpillars hide in leaf nests tied together with silk. Caterpillars overwinter as mature larvae, hiding in their nests in the leaf litter until spring, when they pupate.

AT A GLANCE	
HABITAT:	Open forests
PREDOMINANT COLORS:	Brown and white
SEASON MOST OFTEN SEEN:	Early summer (Horace's); summer – fall (Juvenal's)
MIGRATORY:	No

Common Checkered-Skipper

HOW DO I IDENTIFY THEM? This dainty spread-winged skipper looks like it's bathed in salt and pepper. Its 1- to 1½-inch wings are mottled with a sprinkling of white panes on a dark background, which can vary from rusty to black. Males have blue-gray bodies. Females are black. Above, the white checkers coalesce into a loosely organized band across the middle of the fore- and hindwings. The fringe around the wings is often checked with alternating white and black. Below the butterfly is lighter, showing white furry scales on its face and body. The forewing is darker than the hindwing. When this skipper perches with its wings closed, the forewing collapses behind the hindwing so it's less visible, resulting in a characteristic triangular profile. The well-camouflaged caterpillar, if you happen to find it, has smooth greenish skin, with brown or reddish stripes from head to tail.

WHERE DO I FIND THEM? This little skipper lives throughout North America, using habitats at all altitudes and conditions. It is most abundant in open areas with short vegetation. Common checkered-skippers use fields, pastures, meadows, roadsides, disturbed areas, and gardens. They fly energetically over the vegetation, bouncing from flower to flower and hardly pausing at all. Males patrol and defend small territories, flying out to investigate and chase away butterflies and other insects. As the day wanes, they settle down to roost perched at the tops of tall plants.

WHAT CAN I DO TO ATTRACT THEM? Adults feed on nectar and prefer white-flowered plants in the aster family, such as fleabanes, oxeye daisies, shepherd's needles, and calico asters. They'll also feed on tickseed, beggar's ticks (and other small, yellow flowers in the *Bidens* genus), knapweed, and clovers. Common checkered-skipper caterpillars feed on plants in the mallow family, both native and ornamental, such as hibiscus, swamp mallow, globe mallows, cheeses, and hollyhocks.

LIFECYCLE Caterpillars make folded leaf nests to rest and eat in, which they occupy singly and later pupate in. Adults are active from February through October in the South, producing several broods through the season, and from March through September in the North and at higher elevations, resulting in two or more broods. They are winter-hardy as far north as Pennsylvania, but severe winter weather may kill off a significant percentage of the population. To give them the best chance to survive, leave your flowerbeds, where the caterpillars spend the winter in leaf nests, intact when you do your fall cleanup. In spring, skippers from the South spread north to repopulate their warm-season territory.

AT A GLANCE

HABITAT:	Sunny, open habitats
PREDOMINANT COLORS:	Brown/black and white
SEASON MOST OFTEN SEEN:	Spring through fall
MIGRATORY:	No

Least Skipper

HOW DO I IDENTIFY THEM? Least skippers seem like the tiniest possible creatures that could conceivably be butterflies, with impossibly small wings and short antennae. These skippers belong to the grass skipper group, known for their unique perching posture. They hold their hindwings flat away from their bodies and their forewings at a 45-degree angle, looking a bit like a jet plane ready to take off. The upper side of the least's bright orange hindwings is bordered in black. Below, their forewings are black in the middle and edged in orange. Above, they are mostly orange, with a faint black border. Leasts also perch with their wings closed, their forewing mostly tucked behind the hindwing, showing their white faces and orange hindwings, which fade to pale orange in the middle.

WHERE DO I FIND THEM?   Least skippers live in concentrated populations in wet grasslands in eastern North America. Look for them in meadows, ditches, marshes, and along streams. They easily disappear among the taller grasses and plants, but if you watch along trail edges, you'll be able to spot them. They have a bouncy, unhurried flight, and males patrol to find mates. Follow one until it perches, and then creep as close as you can. Hand lenses or close-focusing binoculars will help you better appreciate this tiny skipper.

WHAT CAN I DO TO ATTRACT THEM?   Least skippers feed on grass as caterpillars. They prefer tall grassy areas instead of low vegetation and have been observed feeding on rice cutgrass (*Leersia oryzoides*), marsh millet (*Zizaniopsis miliacea*), bluegrass (*Poa* spp.), and cultivated rice (*Oryza sativa*). Do not mow or remove dead grass in the fall to leave shelter for caterpillars. Adults feed on nectar. They have very long tongues compared to their body size, so they're able to use flowers of many sizes, but they favor low-growing plants such as verbena, chicory, and wood sorrel, as well as water-loving plants such as pickerelweed, which might be found along the streams and ditches the skippers favor.

LIFECYCLE   Least skippers produce as many as four generations each year, depending on the climate. Further north, they produce fewer generations. They're active from May through October in the North and from February to December in the South. The caterpillars are very small, as you might imagine, and they live alone in nests made by wrapping a single grass blade around themselves tied with silk. The last generation of late-stage caterpillars overwinters, pupating in the spring.

AT A GLANCE	
HABITAT:	Wet grasslands
PREDOMINANT COLORS:	Orange and black
SEASON MOST OFTEN SEEN:	Spring through fall
MIGRATORY:	No

Peck's Skipper

HOW DO I IDENTIFY THEM? The 1-inch peck's skipper, which poses all of the typical grass skipper challenges, provides one lightning fast field mark that will help you recognize it. On the underside of the hindwing are two (sometimes connected) light patches. The outer patch has an extension, like a tooth, poking out toward the rear edge of the wing. Males have dark brown upper wings, and females have crisp orange squares surrounded by black. The mnemonic "Peck's have checks" may help you remember the field marks for this skipper. Some of the black marks on the underside of the hindwing and some of the orange marks on the upper side of the forewing are, in fact, squared enough that they could be considered "checks."

WHERE DO I FIND THEM? Peck's skippers range east from British Columbia in Canada, south through the Midwest and Appalachia, and back north through New England, Nova Scotia, and New Brunswick. They stick to grassy habitats, including lawns, meadows, fields, pastures, roadsides, prairies, and disturbed areas even in urban spaces. They fly quickly for such a small butterfly, but males can often be spotted perching on short vegetation to watch and display for roaming females.

WHAT CAN I DO TO ATTRACT THEM? Peck's skippers visit gardens frequently and feed on nectar as adults. Plant early summer–blooming native plants such as thistles, milkweed, and New Jersey tea. In their southern range, they're active later in the season, so you will want to supplement these flowers with later-blooming plants, including goldenrod, asters, and other plants appropriate to your area. The caterpillars feed on grass, primarily rice cutgrass (*Leersia oryzoides*), and Kentucky bluegrass (*Poa pratensis*). One of the best things you can do to help skippers in your yard is to leave areas of lawn or edges unmowed so that caterpillars can complete their growth cycle. During fall cleanup, leave grasses long through the winter so that the year's last caterpillars can overwinter safely.

LIFECYCLE For such a common butterfly, the life cycle of the Peck's skipper is still mostly a mystery. There hasn't been much research or observation of their mating habits, reproductive strategy, or overwintering needs. They're active in June and July in the North, and it's believed that they produce one or two generations there. In the South, they're active from May through October, likely producing two or three generations each year. Peck's skippers overwinter as larvae and possibly pupae.

AT A GLANCE	
HABITAT:	Grasslands
PREDOMINANT COLORS:	Orange and black
SEASON MOST OFTEN SEEN:	Summer
MIGRATORY:	No

Tawny-Edged Skipper

HOW DO I IDENTIFY THEM?   The tawny-edged skipper is an inconspicuous, plain dark skipper, but the name gives a clue for how to recognize it. The front edge of the forewing both above and below is orange, varying from light and bright to rusty—the "tawny edge"—in contrast to its dull brown upper wings and grayish underwings. They have an approximately 1-inch wingspan, and the upper sides of their wings are dark olive or brown. Females have light checkmarks on their forewings, arranged close to the front edge to form what some call a bracelet that shows through to the underside. The undersides of the wings are dull rusty brown or orange, looking as if they are frosted with gray scales. The crossline skipper, another common skipper whose range overlaps with the tawny-edged, is very similar, but has a short band of small, pale spots on the underside of its hindwing.

WHERE DO I FIND THEM?

They are common east of the Rockies, south through Florida, and north to Nova Scotia. They range through the Great Plains and in some of the wetter areas of the West. Tawny-edged skippers prefer grassy habitats, including lawns, meadows, fields, pastures, roadsides, and prairies, but they avoid disturbed areas, such as city lots. Males perch on low vegetation to display.

WHAT CAN I DO TO ATTRACT THEM?

Adult tawny-edged skippers feed on nectar. Plants such as clover, thistles, milkweed, dogbane, mints, and asters will attract them to your flowerbeds. Caterpillars feed on grasses such as panic grasses—which can take the place of exotic ornamental grasses that are commonly available for landscaping—and bluegrass. Alternatively, you can leave areas of your yard unmowed and seed the areas with native grasses and wildflowers to grow a small meadow for skippers to use. Leave these areas alone during fall cleanup so caterpillars and pupae have shelter through the winter.

LIFECYCLE

Tawny-edged skippers produce one brood in the North, and two or more in the South. They are active through the summer, but may stretch their breeding season longer depending on the climate. Like many common skippers, tawny-edged skippers have not received much attention from researchers, so much of their life cycle is unknown. Caterpillars tie grass blades together with silk to form nests that they occupy singly for protection as well as food. This skipper likely overwinters in its chrysalis, but it might also overwinter as a late-stage caterpillar.

AT A GLANCE	
HABITAT:	Grasslands
PREDOMINANT COLORS:	Orange and black
SEASON MOST OFTEN SEEN:	Summer
MIGRATORY:	No

Dun Skipper

The dun skipper is a very plain, dark, 1-inch skipper, and its *lack* of field marks is one of the best ways to identify it, even though there are plenty of other skipper species who share its nondescript appearance. The dun skipper's forewings are strongly pointed and triangular. Above and below, the wings are a purplish brown, with the suggestion of an orange or bronze gleam in certain light. Some males have rusty orange heads and thoraxes. Females have a group of very small white specks on the forewing, called a bracelet, arranged at what could be considered the "wrist" of the wing. Caterpillars are small, narrow enough to fit between the edges of a grass blade. They are smooth green with yellow- or red-and-black striped eyes.

WHERE DO I FIND THEM?
Dun skippers are usually found in wetlands, but they have also expanded their taste to take advantage of a wide variety of other habitats. Look for dun skippers in meadows, pastures, fields and roadsides, and in marshes, overgrown ditches, and in the vegetation along creeks and streams. They're common throughout the United States east of the Rockies and north around the Great Lakes into southern Canada. They roam further north into Manitoba and Ontario, and they have additional populations in the Northwest, California, and through Texas, but are uncommon outside their core range.

WHAT CAN I DO TO ATTRACT THEM?
The caterpillars of this small, dark skipper feed on a group of grasslike plants called sedges, which thrive in moist and shaded areas and make attractive substitutes for ornamental grasses. Adult dun skippers feed on nectar and seem to show a preference for white, purple, or pink flowers, like those from milkweeds, mints, purple vetch, selfheal, dogbane, and New Jersey tea.

LIFECYCLE
Dun skippers are active all summer long in the North but only produce a single generation each year. They can squeeze out two or more generations further south in their range, where the summer is longer and warmer. Male dun skippers perch on low vegetation to watch and display for passing females, mostly in the afternoon. They may also spend time at puddles, especially right after they emerge from pupation. Caterpillars construct nests by tying sedge blades together with silk. Like most skipper caterpillars, they leave their nests to throw their frass (feces) far beyond their host plant. They overwinter as late-stage caterpillars and pupate in their nests in the spring.

AT A GLANCE	
HABITAT:	Wetlands
PREDOMINANT COLORS:	Brown
SEASON MOST OFTEN SEEN:	Summer
MIGRATORY:	No

Hobomok Skipper

HOW DO I IDENTIFY THEM? The Hobomok skipper is a close relative of the Zabulon skipper, and in some instances the two could easily be confused. However, knowing what to look for will help you distinguish between the two. Hobomok skippers have very rounded wings, and males are orange and brown below, with fore and hindwings bordered in unbroken brown that may be frosted in violet along the edges. The orange patch on the hindwing usually has a slight toothlike extension in the middle. Above, males have thick black borders on fore- and hindwings surrounding smaller orange patches. Females have two forms—an orange-and-brown form that closely resembles the male, though browner overall, and a dark form. The dark female shows the same pattern as the bright female, though in shades of brown instead of orange, with a small scatter of white speckles on the tip of the forewing and sometimes a frosting of violet scales. Caterpillars are light brown or orange with very faint stripes from side to side, covered in short white hairs. Their heads are dark brown and bulbous, separated from the body by a narrow "neck."

WHERE DO I FIND THEM?

The range of Hobomok skippers overlaps that of Zabulons through most of the Midwest and Mid-Atlantic, but stretches further north into Nova Scotia and extends westward through the upper Midwest and into most of Canada. Hobomoks live in woodlands, unlike most members of the grass-skipper group, but can also be found in open fields, gardens, clearings, forest edges, and roads. Males perch and display from shrubs in sunny clearings instead of from grasses.

WHAT CAN I DO TO ATTRACT THEM?

Adults primarily feed on nectar and will visit milkweeds, thistles, clovers, fleabane, viper's bugloss, and verbenas. Like many woodland butterflies, Hobomok skippers will also seek nutrients from animal dung or bird droppings. Plant asters and mints to attract them. Caterpillars feed on panic grasses and bluegrass.

LIFECYCLE

Hobomok skippers produce a single generation during their long active season, which lasts about two months in the early part of summer. Caterpillars make grass nests and feed at night. They also pupate in a grass nest. Like many skippers, it's not known exactly how Hobomok skippers overwinter, though most likely as either larvae or pupae. In either stage, they rely on a thick thatch of grass leaves to shelter and protect them through the cold months.

AT A GLANCE	
HABITAT:	Woodlands
PREDOMINANT COLORS:	Orange and black
SEASON MOST OFTEN SEEN:	Summer
MIGRATORY:	No

Zabulon Skipper

HOW DO I IDENTIFY THEM?   Zabulon and Hobomok skippers have similar colorings, but with a little practice, you'll be able to tell the difference. The wings of Zabulons are more pointed than those of Hobomoks. Males are overall golden-toned: bright yellow wing patches enclosed with black bands above and golden underwings freckled with warm brown dots below. The underside of their hindwing has a brown base where it attaches, enclosing a yellow spot at the front "point" of the hindwing. Female Zabulons are warm purple-brown, very similar to the dark morph of the Hobomok skipper. Above, they have a few glassy panes on their forewings. Below their wings are frosted with gray or lavender. A trace of white edges the top curve of their hindwing, a distinct field mark for female Zabulon skippers. The caterpillars are dull tan or light brown, covered in short white hairs.

WHERE DO I FIND THEM? Zabulons are adapted to a wide variety of habitats. They prefer brushy, overgrown clearings near woods but can also be found roadside, streamside, or in parks and gardens where their host plants are found. They range from the Southeast up into the Mid-Atlantic region. They can roam as far as the Plains, eastern Texas, and south through Central America. Males perch at head height. They may use the same perch throughout their lifetime and gather at puddles with other butterflies.

WHAT CAN I DO TO ATTRACT THEM? Zabulon skippers feed on grasses as caterpillars, especially lovegrass and bluegrasses. They've been documented feeding on many different species, so any native plants used as ornamentals or let grow wild in a wildflower patch may appeal to breeding Zabulons. Adults feed on nectar. Their tongues are quite long, and they feed on many native plants, including milkweed, thistles, buttonbush, and joe-pye weed. Leave your yard, or at least parts of it, covered in fallen leaves and dead vegetation at the end of the growing season so that overwintering caterpillars have shelter through the cold.

LIFECYCLE Zabulon skippers produce two to three generations each year: one early-season generation in the warmth of spring and a second generation in late summer. They are thought to overwinter as caterpillars, though more research is needed to confirm this. Caterpillars make nests, starting with a single grass blade folded over when small, and they graduate to a larger nest of grass leaves tied together, in which they pupate as well.

AT A GLANCE

HABITAT:	Brushy openings
PREDOMINANT COLORS:	Yellow and black
SEASON MOST OFTEN SEEN:	Summer
MIGRATORY:	No

Delaware Skipper

HOW DO I IDENTIFY THEM?   The Delaware skipper is a bright, medium-sized skipper of the East, quite noticeable as it flits by at ankle height flashing its 1¼-inch golden orange wings. The underwings are uniformly orange, without checks or freckles like many other similar skippers. They could be confused with similarly colored least skippers, but they are much larger. Above, the Delaware's orange wings are bordered with black, with a rim of orange fringe around the edge of the wings. Males and females resemble each other, but display subtle differences on the upper side of the wings. The forewings show black veins, heavier on the female, merging into a chevron on the male, and a large black patch enclosing an orange spot—an "eye"—on the female. They perch with their wings closed but also soak up the sun in the typical grass-skipper jet-plane basking posture. Caterpillars are pale green with a black necklace and backward pointing chevron on the rear, as well as black-and-white striped eyes.

WHERE DO I FIND THEM? Delawares live in wet, grassy habitats such as meadows, wet prairies, pond edges, marshes, and bogs, but have also been seen in drier habitats, including pastures, parks, and gardens. They live throughout the eastern United States, from Maine to Florida, and west into Montana and southern Canada. Males perch at about knee height on vegetation and also visit puddles.

WHAT CAN I DO TO ATTRACT THEM? Nectar-feeding adults visit all sorts of flowers, showing a preference for flowers with white and pink petals. Fleabane, common and swamp milkweed, sweet pepperbush, thistles, and pickerelweed (a plant of ponds and lakesides) have all been documented as food sources. Caterpillars, like most grass skippers, feed on grasses such as big bluestem, switchgrass, panic grasses, and beard grass, but may also feed on sedges. They avoid disturbed areas but may visit established gardens. Like many skippers, they benefit from unmowed meadow or natural areas of your yard where they can shelter through the winter.

LIFECYCLE Delaware skippers breed later in the season than many other skippers, from late June through August in the North, though they're active for the entire summer further south. They produce a single generation in the North, two in the South. Like most of the grass skippers, caterpillars wrap themselves in grass-leaf nests. They pupate in their grass nests and overwinter as late-stage caterpillars or pupa sheltering in the grass.

AT A GLANCE	
HABITAT:	Wet grasslands
PREDOMINANT COLORS:	Orange and black
SEASON MOST OFTEN SEEN:	Late summer
MIGRATORY:	No

Beyond the Backyard:
BUTTERFLY
HOTSPOTS

This list only includes a handful of possible destinations for butterfly lovers. Be sure to visit botanical gardens, nature preserves, and parks in your neighborhood to encounter butterflies throughout the year!

Pismo State Beach
(fall and winter)
555 Pier Avenue
Oceano, CA 93445
(805) 473-7220
www.parks.ca.gov/?page_id=595

This popular beach and campground has one major draw for butterfly lovers: it hosts one of the largest winter colonies of monarch butterflies in the United States. Monarchs gather by the thousands in a grove of eucalyptus trees to roost and rest through the winter. Docents are available from November through February to answer questions.

Joseph H. Williams Tallgrass Prairie Preserve
(spring and early summer)
The Nature Conservancy
Tallgrass Prairie Preserve
P.O. Box 458
Pawhuska, OK 74056
(918)287-4803
www.nature.org/ourinitiatives/regions/northamerica/unitedstates/oklahoma/
    placesweprotect/tallgrass-prairie-preserve.xml

The Nature Conservancy manages this 39,000-acre preserve, the largest area of tallgrass prairie remaining in the world. Grazing bison herds and strategic prescribed burns help maintain this threatened ecosystem. In May and June, peak wildflower bloom carpets the prairie with color, attracting a wide variety of butterfly species, including ladies, fritillaries, monarchs, sulphurs, and more. The preserve has a visitor center, a 10-mile driving loop, and two nature trails through several different habitats.

National Butterfly Center
(year-round)
3333 Butterfly Park Drive
Mission, TX 78572
956-583-5400
www.nationalbutterflycenter.org

The National Butterfly Center has earned its reputation as the "Butterfly Capital of the USA," having hosted at least two hundred species of North American butterflies. This 100-acre preserve in the Rio Grande Valley is operated by the North American Butterfly Association and features a visitor center, an extensive native plant butterfly garden, a native plant nursery, and hosts the annual Texas Butterfly Festival in November. Fall visitors are treated to hundreds of species, including concentrations of migrating butterflies heading south for the winter.

New River Gorge National River
(spring through fall)
P.O. Box 246,
Glen Jean, WV 25846
304-574-2115
www.nps.gov/neri

The New River, one of the oldest rivers in North America, cut the New River Gorge through the Appalachian Mountains over a period of millennia. The area used to support coal mining but has since been returned to its natural state as a biologically diverse ecosystem in one of the most scenic areas of the eastern United States. Visit in spring when wild azaleas and rhododendrons explode in color, and wildflowers bloom quietly in the glens and forests, attracting dozens of species of butterflies. In the late summer, swallowtails are abundant over and around the river. The annual New River Birding and Nature Festival in May focuses on birds primarily, but also offers knowledgeable guides and field trips into prime spring butterfly habitats.

Great Florida Birding and Wildlife Trail
(year-round)
Various locations throughout Florida
www.floridabirdingtrail.com

The state of Florida hosts a wild kaleidoscope of butterflies year-round, and they are everywhere. The Great Florida Birding and Wildlife Trail connects 2,000 miles of protected habitat in over five hundred locations throughout the state. Use the website to search for habitats, parks, and preserves where you'll be sure to find butterflies while you visit.

Coastal Maine Botanical Garden

(spring and summer)
132 Botanical Gardens Drive
Boothbay, ME 04537
(207) 633-8000
www.mainegardens.org

This 250-acre waterfront garden offers natural and cultivated gardens, natural trails, and flowers and butterflies galore. Native plants are incorporated throughout the gardens, providing inspiration for butterfly gardeners who wish to support butterflies and other pollinators. Thanks to dedicated horticulturalists who plan and maintain the garden for beauty and blooms all season, the Coastal Maine Botanical Garden offers plenty of opportunities to admire butterflies.

Cape May Point State Park

(fall)
P.O. Box 107
Cape May Point, NJ 08212
(609) 884-2159
www.state.nj.us/dep/parksandforests/parks/capemay.html

Cape May in New Jersey is one of the best places on the East Coast to catch fall butterfly migration. New Jersey tapers to a narrow peninsula at its southernmost point, which concentrates southbound migrants of both the feathered and fluttery kind, including monarchs and other migrating butterflies. There are several parks and preserves in the area; Cape May Point State Park is a great place to start, with its scenic lighthouse, wheelchair-accessible trails, and a variety of coastal habitats. In October and November, monarchs cluster in low pine trees to roost for the night on their way south. If you can't get there to see the roosts, hike the trails and watch dozens, if not hundreds, of monarchs shoot by throughout the day.

RESOURCES

ORGANIZATIONS

Bird Watcher's Digest
P.O. Box 110
Marietta, OH 45750
www.birdwatchersdigest.com

Butterflies and Moths of North America
www.butterfliesandmoths.org

Lady Bird Johnson Wildflower Center
4801 La Crosse Avenue
Austin, TX 78739
www.wildflower.org

The Monarch Joint Venture
University of Minnesota
Department of Fisheries, Wildlife,
    and Conservation Biology
2003 Upper Buford Circle
135 Skok Hall
St. Paul, MN 55108
www.monarchjointventure.org

North American Butterfly Association
4 Delaware Avenue
Morristown, NJ 07960
www.naba.org

North American Native Plant Society
NANPS
P.O. Box 84, Station D
Toronto, ON M9A 4X1
Canada
www.nanps.org

Pollinator Partnership
423 Washington Street, 5th Floor
San Francisco, CA 94111
www.pollinator.org

The Nature Conservancy
4245 North Fairfax Drive, Suite 100
Arlington, VA 22203-1606
www.nature.org

Xerces Societ
628 NE Broadway Suite 200
Portland, OR 97232
www.xerces.org

PERIODICALS FOR BUTTERFLY WATCHERS

American Butterflies
North American Butterfly Association,
    Inc. (NABA)
4 Delaware Road
Morristown, NJ 07960
www.naba.org/pubs/abm.html

Birds and Blooms
1610 North 2nd Street, Suite 102
Milwaukee, WI 53212
www.birdsandblooms.com

Butterfly Gardener
North American Butterfly Association,
    Inc. (NABA)
4 Delaware Road
Morristown, NJ 07960
www.naba.org/pubs/bg.html

INDEX

MEET ERIN GETTLER

Erin Gettler is a naturalist, writer, photographer, and artist with a deep love for the ecological treasures found in urban areas and suburban backyards. She developed her curiosity for the natural world in her own childhood suburban neighborhood, between afternoons spent in trees and gardens, and hours buried in encyclopedias and field guides. That childhood infatuation only deepened as she started seeking out the green places on maps, encountering parks and preserves full of birds and butterflies in real life, off the pages. As a grownup, she bookends her days and weeks exploring Long Island from end to end and fork to fork, sketching and photographing birds, butterflies, plants, and whales.

PHOTO CREDITS